Washington and Ohio Railroad Company

The Washington and Ohio Railroad

A glance at the country through which it passes, between Washington, D.

C., and the Ohio River

Washington and Ohio Railroad Company

The Washington and Ohio Railroad
*A glance at the country through which it passes, between Washington, D. C., and
the Ohio River*

ISBN/EAN: 9783744735711

Printed in Europe, USA, Canada, Australia, Japan

Cover: Foto ©ninafisch / pixelio.de

More available books at **www.hansebooks.com**

WASHINGTON AND OHIO

RAILROAD.

A GLANCE AT THE COUNTRY THROUGH WHICH IT PASSES,

BETWEEN

WASHINGTON, D. C.,

AND

THE OHIO RIVER,

A DISTANCE OF

325 MILES.

PHILADELPHIA:

COLLINS, PRINTER, 705 JAYNE STREET.

1873.

WASHINGTON AND OHIO RAIL ROAD.

OFFICERS AND DIRECTORS.

President.

LEWIS McKENZIE, Alexandria, Va.

Clerk and Treasurer.

REUBEN JOHNSTON. Alexandria, Va.

Chief Engineer.

WASHINGTON BLYTHE. Alexandria, Va.

General Superintendent.

R. H. HAVENER. Alexandria, Va.

Directors,

CASSIUS F. LEE,	Alexandria, Va.
ANDREW JAMIESON,	Alexandria, Va.
CHARLES B. BALL,	Leesburg, Va.
HENRY HEATON,	Leesburg, Va.
BENJAMIN MORGAN,	Berryville, Va.
RICHARD HENRY LEE,	Millwood, Va.
F. W. M. HOLLIDAY,	Winchester, Va.

CONTENTS.

PAGE

THE WASHINGTON AND OHIO RAIL ROAD.

—

THE WASHINGTON AND OHIO RAIL ROAD COMPANY, a corporation originally chartered by the General Assembly of Virginia under the title of "The Alexandria, Loudoun, and Hampshire Rail Road Company," was at first intended to extend *only* from the city of Alexandria, in the State of Virginia, to the coal fields of Hampshire, then in said State, now a county of West Virginia, a distance of about 180 miles. But the great importance of a through and direct connection across the States of Virginia and West Virginia, between the Ohio River on the west, and the city of Washington,

THE NATIONAL CAPITAL,

with its commodious roadstead at Alexandria, Va., on the east, induced this company to apply to the Legislature of the State of West Virginia for authority to extend its line through that State to the most suitable point within its limits on the Ohio.

The Legislature of West Virginia, on the 19th day of February, 1870, passed "an act" conferring upon this company the necessary authority "to extend and construct their railroad from the line of the State of Virginia, westwardly, through the State of West Virginia, to the west bank of the Ohio River at any point between the Little Kanawha and the Big Sandy Rivers, and to connect said railroad, by branches, with the Chesapeake and Ohio Rail Road and with the Baltimore and Ohio Rail Road, and to construct such other branches, not to exceed fifty miles in length in any one case, as might be deemed expedient."

Under this authority, the Washington and Ohio Rail Road Company caused the necessary surveys to be made, and, on the report of its engineers, decided upon Point Pleasant, in Mason County, as the most advantageous location for its terminus on the Ohio, a distance of 325 miles from tide-water on the Potomac at Washington and Alexandria.

2

THE ROUTE OF "THE WASHINGTON AND OHIO RAIL ROAD," AND THE RESOURCES OF THE COUNTRY THROUGH WHICH IT WILL PASS.

THE WASHINGTON AND OHIO RAIL ROAD, commencing at the city of Alexandria, taps the Alexandria and Washington Rail Road one and a half miles from Alexandria, by which *all rail* connection is made with the city of Washington, five miles distant, and by which means the transportation of freight and passengers is secured, daily, to and from the National Capital without change of cars.

From the junction of the Washington and Ohio, and the Alexandria and Washington Rail Roads, the Washington and Ohio Rail Road passes for twenty-five miles through the counties of Alexandria and Fairfax, draining an area of one hundred and fifty square miles. This portion of the line is being rapidly settled by purchasers from the Northern and Western States, and from Europe, and is being much improved. It thence runs for twenty-eight miles through the county of Loudoun, with a tributary territory of three hundred square miles, and passing by Leesburg, the county-seat, a town of nearly two thousand inhabitants. Many new settlers have purchased lands in this county since 1866, and it is estimated that the population is now about twenty-five thousand. Besides being one of the most productive agricultural counties in the State, it has large deposits of limestone, marble, iron, and other minerals, only needing facilities of transportation to render the working of them very remunerative. New turnpikes, and a branch railroad from Leesburg to Aldie, are in progress of development, which will add largely to the productive capacity of the county.

A deposit of marble, of almost inexhaustible quantity, has been recently discovered, of a quality equal to the finest Italian, and a company has been chartered for working it on a large scale. This marble is only fifty miles from Washington City, and will be delivered from the quarry to any building site in that city without change of cars.

Leaving the western line of Loudoun County, the line enters Clarke County at the summit of the Blue Ridge, and traverses the county, in nearly a western direction, for fifteen miles. This is the finest wheat and corn growing county in the State, is well adapted to grazing, and has large and valuable deposits of iron ore of fine quality.

The county of Jefferson, adjoining Clarke County on the north, will be largely drained by this road. Leaving Clarke County, the line traverses Frederick County for about twenty-five miles, crosses the Valley Rail Road within a mile of the town of Winchester, or will pass through the town, and must successfully compete for a large share of the products of the Shenandoah Valley.

Frederick County has nearly fifty flouring mills, and several successful woollen mills, and the town of Winchester is becoming an important manufacturing centre for agricultural and other machinery. In this county are seventy-five thousand acres of limestone land, capable of producing a million bushels of wheat; and there are eight turnpike roads, connecting these lands with the town of Winchester. The population of Winchester is about five thousand, and the distance to Washington by this line only seventy-five miles, against one hundred and thirty-seven miles by the present route of the Baltimore and Ohio Rail Road.

After leaving Winchester, the line passes through Petticoat Gap, in the Little North Mountain, and reaches the summit of the Great North Mountain at Lockhart's Gap with easy grades, crossing with an open cut of about twenty feet, and thence on, by Capper's Spring, now called "Rock Enon," and Capon Springs, to the county of Hampshire, in West Virginia.

Capon Springs, in the productive valley of the Cacapon River, are thirty miles from Winchester, and one mile from the line of this road. These springs are too well known as a place of resort to require a special description; but when brought within four hours' ride of the National Capital, being only ninety-five miles distant, will be greatly in repute. Capper's (Rock Enon) Spring, on the same side of the mountain, and five miles nearer to Washington, is second to none in the State for its medicinal qualities, though now comparatively unknown. These springs are destined to rival, successfully, the most popular of our watering places.

Leaving Capon Springs, and passing through the Valley to a point one and a half miles beyond the town of Wardensville, the line will pass through Sandy Ridge by one of the grandest and most picturesque gaps in the mountains of Virginia. Near this point the famous Lost River disappears, running under the mountain for two and a half miles, and reappearing as the Great Cacapon River. Following the Valley of Lost River and its tributary streams, the South Branch Mountain is reached, and crossing by a tunnel, and descending the western slope, we arrive at the town of Moorefield, the county seat of Hardy, in the Great South Branch Valley. This Valley is five hundred feet lower than the Valley of Lost River, and, having an alluvial soil of great depth, is of unsurpassed fertility. Corn has been grown on the same lands for a hundred consecutive years, without apparently diminishing the yield; and this splendid region is only needing a proper outlet for its productions, to become justly far-famed. From Moorefield the Baltimore and Ohio Rail Road is distant on the north nearly fifty miles; and the nearest railroad on the south is the Chesapeake and Ohio, distant more than one hundred miles.

Leaving the Valley of the South Branch, and crossing several minor valleys and ridges, the Alleghany Mountains are reached, and passed with a tunnel; near which point a most splendid panorama is presented. Looking eastward, the whole country, from Harper's Ferry on the north, to the Peaks of Otter on the south, is spread out in one grand view, every range of mountain being clearly seen and distinctly marked, and the pen of the most imaginative writer would fail to overdraw the picture: while to the south and southwest, the view is, if possible, more grand, though less extensive.

On the western slope of the Alleghany, the first coal is reached—distant from Washington City one hundred and eighty miles; and from this point to the Ohio River, valuable beds, from three to twenty feet in thickness, are found, in every county of West Virginia through which the line will pass, viz.: Tucker, Randolph, Barbour, Upshur, Lewis, Gilmer, Calhoun, Roane, Jackson, and Mason. These coals are of a bituminous character, and most of them the best gas-coal in the country, furnishing an illimitable supply, and very cheaply worked. In the valleys of the head-waters of the Cheat River, known as Dry Fork, Laurel Fork, Shaver's Fork, and Glade Fork, are found forests of the original growth of oak, pine, chestnut, poplar, walnut, maple, cherry, and other woods, of the finest quality and in immense quantities. In Glade Fork may be seen forty odd poplars on an acre, thirty of which will measure an average of eighty feet without a limb—many of them a hundred—straight as a gun-barrel, and five feet through the butt. At other points, where the cherry trees preponderate, an acre may be selected having on it twenty cherry trees which will measure fifty feet to the first limb, are perfectly straight, and three feet through the stump, and apparently (to the eye) as large at fifty feet from the ground as at three feet. There is, in a single cove of the mountains, a group of sugar maples containing more than five thousand trees of large size. The oak and pine timber is not excelled in quality by that of any other region in the United States, many of the pines being more than two hundred feet high, and six feet thick. The entire country, from the mountains to the Ohio River, is covered with equally fine timber. The iron ore of this region is abundant, and of the best quality, and water power, immense and convenient, would furnish the means of driving rolling mills and other factories unnumbered.

From the Cheat River, in Randolph County, the line traverses the counties named above, and reaches the Ohio River without a tunnel or serious obstruction, on a distance of one hundred and fifty miles.

All the country west of the mountains abounds in coal and iron, and the most valuable timber, besides being one of the best natural grass regions anywhere to be found. The soil is clay, naturally under-drained, and the hills do not wash. Cattle are kept unhoused, and grazed throughout the year, only requiring hay when the snow prevents them from reaching the pasturage, which rarely happens. Blue grass is indigenous, and timothy grows most luxuriantly. The oil wells in Wirt and other counties are very productive, and many others would be opened if proper outlets existed to market. The region known as the " Eternal Centre " produces thousands of barrels of oil per day, and would furnish a very profitable employment for a railroad. In Mason County, containing four hundred and thirty square miles, all of which is tillable land, about one-fourth is productive bottom land, worth an average of fifty dollars an acre for farming purposes. In this county is a good coal field, now being extensively worked, and numerous salt wells, turning out, for nine furnaces, seven thousand bushels per day. In the county of Lewis, with seventeen hundred and three male inhabitants over twenty-one years of age, but one-seventh of the arable land is cleared.

The distance from Washington City and Alexandria, by this line, to the Ohio River, is three hundred and twenty-five miles, and to Cincinnati, via a projected line from Point Pleasant, four hundred and seventy-five miles. To Chicago, seven hundred and twenty miles; and to Memphis, via Winchester and Danville, Kentucky, eight hundred and eighty miles; shortening the distance over the shortest present routes—to Cincinnati, one hundred and thirty-five miles; to Chicago, one hundred and twenty-two miles; and to Memphis, fifty-four miles. The road is now finished to Hamilton, in Loudoun County, forty-four miles from Washington, and supporting two daily passenger trains and one freight train each way, and is now being pressed forward to Snickersville, eleven miles beyond.

This hasty glance of the route of the Washington and Ohio Rail Road affords but a faint idea, not only of its value as a means for the transportation of passengers and freights, but for the development of the immense wealth of the mountains and valleys of West Virginia, and the great valley of the Mississippi.

This company is desirous to prosecute its work to final completion at the earliest practicable period, but its limited means have retarded its operations.

The funds required for its building, so far as completed, were furnished by the State and people of Virginia; and the interest of the people residing in the counties, and those contiguous thereto, along its line, in the State of West Virginia, is shown by their county subscriptions, in making which they prudently and properly provided that they should be available only as the road reached their respective limits.

To enable this company to take advantage of these subscriptions the city of Washington has been invited to make a subscription of one million dollars to its capital stock, said subscription to be made in the bonds of the city, running thirty years, with interest thereon at the rate of six per centum per annum, payable half yearly; the said sum of one million dollars to be delivered to this company at the rate of sixteen thousand dollars for each and every mile of railroad actually completed, to the satisfaction of the authorities of said city, and certificates for the tax to be issued, so that the actual tax payer might finally become the owner of the stock, a provision which, this company thinks, ought to commend itself to the government and people of Washington. A large portion of the substantial citizens of Washington (property holders and business men), assured of the great advantages which will result to their city by the building of this line, gave their assent to said subscription in a petition to the Congress of the United States, and in which the necessary authority was asked to enable them to make the subscription requested by this company. A bill for this purpose was subsequently introduced in the House of Delegates of the District of Columbia, but the Legislative Assembly adjourned without taking final action upon it.

The importance of this road to the city of Washington, as opening up a new and shorter route, over those existing or projected, by fifty-four, fifty-eight, and ninety-five miles respectively, nearer to tide from the west and southwest, passing through a country abounding in coal, iron, minerals of all descriptions, timber of immense value, and furnishing to the federal metropolis every description of agricultural production, thus reducing the price of living, makes it of the first importance that the city of Washington should co-operate in this great enterprise; and whilst the city of Alexandria, with its fine depth of water, and its other facilities for the accommodation of a heavy business, must control, in a great measure, the bulk of the coal trade,

Washington, as the seat of the General Government, will attract the heavy passenger traffic which the Washington and Ohio Rail Road will command.

Out of the subscription of one million dollars requested from the city of Washington, it is the purpose of this company to build an independent line of road to that city from the most suitable and convenient point on its present line.

Attention is called to the sketches of the several counties in Virginia and West Virginia through which the Washington and Ohio Rail Road will pass—showing character of soil, climate, minerals, timbers, water powers, adaptation to the culture of fruit, grapes, etc.

Parties seeking investments in fine farming lands, grazing lands, water powers, timbered tracts, coal and iron lands, in the manufacture of salt, and in the culture of the various kinds of fruit produced in this fine climate, will not fail to see in the country through which this road will pass a most inviting field for safe and profitable investment. Letters of inquiry from parties who may desire more minute information on these subjects, will receive prompt attention by addressing the President of this company.

The people along the line are anxious for immigration, and gladly extend a cordial welcome to all, whether from the States of the Union, Great Britain, or the continent of Europe. In this connection reference is made to the Allan Line of Steamers as affording regular facilities for the transportation of passengers between Liverpool, England, and the cities of Alexandria and Washington, *via* Norfolk, Virginia.

For the information of parties who may desire to co-operate in the building of this great line it is proper to state the financial condition of the Washington and Ohio Rail Road on the 30th of September, 1872, the end of the last fiscal year.

The line of road from Alexandria to Hamilton Station, forty-four miles, including a short link connecting the Washington and Ohio Rail Road with the Alexandria and Washington, a large and substantial two-story brick passenger depot and frame shedding, large brick freight depot, round house for locomotives, repair shops, car shops, and other buildings, turn-table, etc., occupying a square of ground covering two acres, and three squares of ground (six acres) immediately adjacent, with a water front of eight hundred and thirty-eight feet, conveniently situated at Alexandria; passenger and freight houses at Fall's Church, Vienna, Thornton, Herndon, Guilford, Farmwell, Leesburg, Clark's Gap, and Hamilton stations, including turn-tables at Leesburg and Hamilton, cost about the sum of $1,800,000, the supposed present value of which is $1,335,000 00

Liabilities, including $130,400 00, of
   the W. & O. R. R. bonds at par $528,529 77
Deduct good assets on hand   .   . 123,731 82
                                  $104,797 95

Leaving as security for the bond-
   holders the sum of   .   .   .   930,202 05
                                    $1,335,000 00

CINCINNATI CHAMBER OF COMMERCE.

In order to show the interest mainifested in this great work by the Chamber of Commerce of the city of Cincinnati, and of the Board of Trade of the city of Washington, the resolutions adopted by these bodies are hereto annexed.

THE WASHINGTON AND OHIO RAIL ROAD—REPORT TO CHAMBER OF COMMERCE—INDORSEMENT OF THE PROJECT—SPEECH OF COL. WM. H. TRIMBLE.*

At the close of business hours on 'Change yesterday, the Committee to whom was submitted the subject of the Washington and Ohio Rail Road, submitted the following report, which was unanimously adopted:—

CHAS. W. ROWLAND,
    President of Cincinnati Chamber of Commerce:—

Your Committee, appointed to report on the subject of certain communications presented by Dr. James C. Hill, of Alexandria, Virginia, showing the Washington and Ohio Rail Road to be a more direct route than any other to the tide-waters of the Potomac from the Ohio River, beg leave to say that they have examined this subject as carefully as was possible without the actual surveys, and find the statements relative to the road to be substantially correct; that it is the most direct route built or projected, and possesses some advantages for this city that no other railroad to the Atlantic seaboard has; and in recommending it to the favorable consideration of this body, and the business community of this section of the State and city, we are governed by the same reasons that induced a former committee of this chamber to report favorably on the Virginia water-line between the Ohio and James rivers, which report received your most cordial indorsement.

The Washington and Ohio Rail Road, as projected and surveyed to

* From Daily Cincinnati Enquirer of 27th October, 1870.

Point Pleasant, on the Ohio River, when completed, will tend to the development and support of certain projected and existing improvements in which Cincinnati and other western cities are mutually interested. When brought to this city, it will give a more direct communication to St. Louis and other western cities than they now have to the seaboard. Chicago will continue her existing relations with this city, because it will give a more direct outlet for her products than can be had by any other route. It will give the shortest railway communication between the Ohio River and the tide-waters of the Potomac, at a point that is of mutual importance to all the country interested in the water-line, commencing at the mouth of the Kanawha River. At the mouth of this stream the great bulk of the future business of the West on the navigable streams of the same will be concentrated, and it is important that a main trunk line railway should be built from this point to the Atlantic seaboard. Nature has placed them so connectedly as to give all these points an almost air-line, and in a central position to the whole country. St. Louis, Cincinnati, Point Pleasant—in other words, the Mississippi, the Ohio, and the Potomac —will be connected and linked in business relations by the building of this road, on a line mutually beneficial to all.

It will give to our commerce and manufactures the most important outlet to the Atlantic seaboard, because the shortest railway transportation, being only three hundred and forty miles,* from the mouth of the Kanawha to Washington City and Alexandria on the Potomac; the depth of water at the latter place being enough for all practical purposes, with an abundance of cheap coal for the use of steamship lines, making it eminently adapted as a point for oceanic communication with the outside world. Being more inland than any other port, it is susceptible of being made more defensible in time of war, which is a matter worthy of consideration. The railway accommodations at the starting point, Alexandria, are, and bid fair to be, of unsurpassed importance. Other connections and intersections of a valuable character will be had when the road is built and finished to Point Pleasant. It passes through a country unsurpassed for health, beauty, and fertility, and abounds in timber, coal, iron, marble, slate, granite, and many other products of forest, field, and garden too numerous to mention. The greater portion of it passes through a region of country not tributary to any other road, and is consequently not running a tilt against any existing improvement. In its course it touches on

* The committee here erroneously make the distance exceed by 15 miles that given by our engineers.

14

several important towns and cities, and runs almost equally distant
between the Chesapeake and Ohio and Baltimore and Ohio Rail
Roads. To the former it must ultimately be of great benefit for its
northern freight and travel.

We herewith furnish a tabular statement of distances of the Washington and Ohio Rail Road, as prepared by the engineer, and as
published in the *Daily Commercial* of the 17th instant; also some
approximated distances, as published in the *Daily Gazette* of the 12th
instant, and the *Enquirer* of the 19th instant, on the distances of
various ports of entry from Cincinnati:—

Your Committee, after a careful examination of the claims of the
Washington and Ohio Rail Road, as presented by her representative,
Dr. Hill, beg leave to offer the following resolutions for the adoption
of this Chamber:—

Resolved, That cheap and quick transportation for the products of
the interior of the country to the tide-waters of the Potomac and
Chesapeake, is not only a necessity, but is demanded by the highest
considerations of an enlightened public policy.

Resolved, That, to secure this, additional direct lines of railways to
the East, in which this city should have a controlling influence, are im-
peratively demanded, not only as a means of procuring cheap freights,
but of protecting our commerce generally from discriminations prejudicial to it.

Resolved, That it will be to the interests of this city and section of
the State, that every encouragement, both private and public, be extended to forward the completion of the shortest and most central
railway to this city from the tide-waters of the Potomac, and the
capital of the United States.

All of which is most respectfully submitted.

JAMES F. TORRENCE,
S. V. REID.
JEFF. BUCKINGHAM,
A. W. MULLEN.

WASHINGTON BOARD OF TRADE—ANNUAL MEETING.*

The annual meeting of the Washington Board of Trade was held
at the rooms of the board last night, S. Bacon, Esq., President, in
the chair.

After a few preliminaries had been adjusted,

Mr. Bacon, from the committee to inquire into the propriety of re-

* From *Patriot*, Washington, January 21, 1871.

commending to Congress the passage of an act to submit to the vote of the citizens of Washington the question whether they will consent to subscribe to the capital stock of the Washington and Ohio Rail Road Company, to the extent of $1,000,000, submitted the following report:—

The committee to whom was referred at the last meeting of the board the action of the Board of Trade of the city of Cincinnati, relative to the Washington and Ohio Rail Road, report:—

That they have carefully examined the whole subject committed to their charge, and do, without hesitation, report that the interests of this city and section have, in the speedy completion of this road to the West, a greater importance than any subject that has ever been before us for action. We believe that the completion of this road to Cincinnati, from whence diverge railroads in every direction, will have the same effect on the future prosperity of Washington and the adjoining cities that the Baltimore and Ohio Road has had upon Baltimore, the Pennsylvania Central upon Philadelphia, and the Erie on New York: for it is a fixed fact that all the cities of this country that have had the enterprise to build railroads to connect with the teeming West have prospered in a ratio several hundred per cent. faster than those who have laid dormant.

We are happy to state that this locality is fast becoming the centre of more than one line of railroad; that we shall soon have, your committee are assured, additional communication with the South by means of the Washington, Fredericksburg and Richmond Rail Road, with the West by way of the Metropolitan Rail Road, and with the East by means of the Potomac Rail Road; and if the proper exertion is made to bring this subject before the people of this city, and all due diligence is made to complete this road to Cincinnati, we believe it will be of more advantage to the city than all the rest of the roads before mentioned. The indorsement of the Chamber of Commerce of the Queen City, and their examination and knowledge of the advantages that will grow out of its completion to this city, is one of the best guarantees that this board can have of the feasibility of its completion and the great interests in the subject.

Your committee has also examined House Bill No. 1724, and the accompanying memorial to the Senate of the United States, praying for the passage of the same; also the bill prepared for the subsequent action of the City Councils, and find that the provision therein made contains ample guarantees to protect the interests of the tax-payers of this city, the largest and most influential number of whom have already signed said memorial. This is sufficient evidence to your committee that they are alive to the interests and future development of this city, and in recommending the passage of this bill they are but reiterating the already expressed wish of the people. This will be simply placing this community in the position to decide for themselves this important measure, which, when completed, will give a permanently increasing value to all property in this locality, which is now to some extent affected by the want of facilities for commercial intercourse with the heart of the great West. Your committee, therefore, submit this report, with the following resolutions.

(Signed)   SAMUEL BACON,
                         J. W. THOMPSON,
                         WM. G. METZEROTT,
                         JOHN W. BOTELER,
                         W. H. CLAGETT.

Be it resolved, That, in view of the facts set forth in this report, it is for the best interest of this city to encourage, by every means at the disposition of the citizens thereof, the speedy completion of the Washington and Ohio Rail Road from this city to the Ohio River, and thence to the city of Cincinnati.

Resolved, That every effort be made to assist, as far as our limited means will enable us, Cincinnati and other western cities in the speedy completion of this, to them, to us, and to the nation, important short-line improvement in communication with the capital of the nation.

Resolved, That it is the best interest of this city that the Senate of the United States pass House Bill No. 1724, granting permission to decide, by a two-thirds vote at a general election, the propriety of subscribing to the capital stock of the said Washington and Ohio Rail Road.

On motion, the report was accepted, and the resolutions adopted.

On motion by Mr. Hall, a vote of thanks was tendered to Dr. J. C. Hill, of Alexandria, Va., for his assistance in furnishing statistics and data to the committee for their report on the Washington and Ohio Rail Road.

WASHINGTON, D. C.,

Is situated near the head of tide-water, and of navigation, on the Potomac, one of the broadest and most beautiful rivers in the Union. It contains many splendid public buildings, those erected for the accommodation of the government being grand and imposing.

The Executive Mansion, the official residence of the President. occupies an elevated position 44 feet above the level of the Potomac. The Capitol is on an eastern eminence, 72 feet above tide, one mile from the President's house. The War and Navy Departments are at the west end of the President's Park, and the Treasury on its eastern line ; the Patent Office, and the General Post Office Departments and the City Hall occupy central locations. The Smithsonian Institution, the National Armory, the Department of Agriculture, the Botanical Gardens, and the Arsenal lie south of " the Avenue," and the Navy Yard and Marine Barracks at the extreme eastern limit of the city. The Army Medical Museum (Late Ford's Theatre) is of great interest to the public, as being the scene of the assassination of President Lincoln.

Washington contains many fine parks, or extensive pleasure grounds. That surrounding the executive residence is beautifully ornamented ; the Capitol Park, although extensive, is now being enlarged. The Smithsonian Institution grounds contain about 50 acres, the Arsenal grounds have an extensive river front, and are growing in beauty. The National Observatory, one mile west of the President's, has its park, and besides these there are numerous reservations which have been tastefully improved, and contribute to the comfort and health of the metropolis.

Washington is not without memorials in honor of the statesmen and patriots of the country; among these may be mentioned the equestrian statues of Washington and Jackson, and the monument to the memory of Lincoln.

The District of Columbia was formed by Act of Congress of the 16th July, 1790. That portion which constitutes its present limits was ceded for that purpose to the United States by the State of Maryland.

The corner-stone of the Capitol was laid by Washington (then President) Sept. 18, 1793, and in 1800 the seat of government was removed from the city of Philadelphia.

Compared with the great capitals of Europe, Washington is still in its infancy. In 1800 its population was but 3210; in 1810 it was 8208; in 1820, 13.247; in 1830, 18.826; in 1840, 23.364; in 1850, 40.001; in 1860, 61,122 ; and in 1870 it had reached 109,199; and as the seat of the general government its future increase of population will be commensurate with the growth of the country.

In the adornment of its avenues and streets vast sums of money have been expended and thousands of mechanics and laborers are now employed in their improvement. The city has many fine drives, and as the seat of the National Government. Washington has drawn to it, and will continue to attract, as permanent residents, citizens from all parts of the country.

As the capital of a great nation, Washington should enjoy superior railroad facilities. It is directly on the great line of travel from the north to the south, and in these directions the present lines afford the necessary accommodations. There is, however, no western outlet, and this inconvenience and impediment to the prosperity of this section of the country has long been experienced.

Starting from the city of Washington and running in a western direction the Washington and Ohio Rail Road makes nearly *an air line* in its passage to the CENTRAL WEST, through a country abounding in all the resources of productive wealth. Such a vast outlet to trade and business ought not to remain closed, and the importance of the early extension of the road will doubtless receive the attention of the city authorities and people.

GEORGETOWN, D. C.,

lies west of Washington, and is connected with it by permanent bridges over Rock Creek, a narrow stream. It is a place of considerable commercial importance on the Potomac at the head of navigation.

By the Chesapeake and Ohio Canal it enjoys a heavy trade in coal from Cumberland, Maryland. It has several large flouring mills, and a population of 11,384.

Partaking of the spirit of its enterprising neighbor, Georgetown is rapidly increasing its wealth and importance.

ALEXANDRIA, VA.

This city is situated on the west bank of the Potomac River, one hundred miles from the Chesapeake Bay, into which it flows, and two hundred miles from the Atlantic Ocean. It is one of the chief cities of Virginia, and is one hundred and nine miles by rail from the city of Richmond, the capital of the State.

The streets are paved, well graded, and cross each other at right angles. It is lighted with gas, is abundantly supplied with pure water, and for health is not surpassed by any other city in the United States. From its elevated grounds on the west it commands an extensive and beautiful view of the surrounding country and of the city of Washington, six miles distant, with which city and Georgetown it has hourly communication by steamboat and railroad.

In 1860 its population was 10,000. This in 1870 had reached

13,570, and its estimated population now (1873) is fully 16,000, which a growing trade is steadily increasing.

As a commercial point Alexandria enjoys great advantages. Twenty-five years ago the products of the country tributary to it were brought to market by means of farm wagons and small vessels; but, with the introduction of railroads, these means of transportation have. to a great extent, passed away, and to accommodate the constantly increasing productions of the country the capacity of several lines of railway are heavily taxed.

It has a fine harbor, the Potomac opposite the city being one mile wide, and from thirty to fifty feet deep, and being supplied with large and commodious wharves, and extensive warehouses afford all the facilities required for commercial purposes.

It has several lines of railway, a canal, turnpikes, and steam communication with Baltimore, Philadelphia, New York, Boston, and Norfolk. At Norfolk connection is made with the ALLAN LINE OF OCEAN STEAMERS to Liverpool, via Halifax, Nova Scotia, and Queenstown, Ireland.

It imports all the salt required for the Potomac fisheries and for interior consumption, the large quantities of lump plaster required for agricultural purposes; and, on the completion of the railway lines now in course of construction, there is no reason why, in addition to these, most of the supplies required for this market, and now imported from foreign countries through other ports, should not be imported from the producing countries directly into Alexandria.

The building of a street railway, to pass through the main business street of the city, from the Washington steamboat wharf, and near the depots of all the railroads running through and out of Alexandria, with a terminus outside of its western limits, will be commenced early in the spring, and completed by the first of July of the present year (1873).

THE WASHINGTON AND OHIO RAIL ROAD,

When completed to the Ohio, will bring the vast trade and travel of that region to the Potomac at Alexandria and Washington. This road is now in operation to Hamilton, Loudoun County, forty-four miles from Alexandria, and over this short line the demands of the country require the running of two daily passenger trains and one freight train each way.

THE ORANGE, ALEXANDRIA, AND MANASSAS RAIL ROAD.

One of the great improvements of the State, has its terminus at Alexandria. This great public work is completed and in successful operation to the city of Lynchburg, in Virginia, one hundred and seventy-one miles southwest from Alexandria, where it connects with the Virginia and Tennessee Rail Road, which has extensive railway connections with the States of Tennessee, Arkansas, Georgia, Alabama, and other States South.

In addition to two branches owned by this road, one running to Warrenton, in Fauquier County, 50 miles from Alexandria, and one to Harrisonburg, Rockingham County, 139 miles from Alexandria, the Orange, Alexandria, and Manassas Rail Road is now building, and will shortly complete, a railroad from Lynchburg, its present terminus, to Danville, in Pittsylvania County, 65½ miles south from Lynchburg, through a rich country, in which the whistle of the locomotive has never been heard.

From Danville it is proposed to extend this road to Statesville, an important point in the State of North Carolina, on the Western North Carolina Rail Road, by which route the Orange, Alexandria, and Manassas Rail Road will form connections with all the railroads in that direction, through the State of North Carolina, to South Carolina, Georgia, Florida, etc.

With the completion of the Danville connection, the Orange, Alexandria, and Manassas Rail Road will own and operate 356½ miles of railway; and it is due to the management to say that no great road in the United States is better, if as well, managed.

THE ALEXANDRIA AND FREDERICKSBURG RAILWAY.

This road was completed and put in operation within the past six months, and by it Alexandria and Washington and the cities north of them enjoy additional rail communication with the city of Richmond and points south. This line passes through the lower eastern sections of the tide-water counties of Fairfax and Prince William, which have heretofore never had any railroad facilities whatever, and, while greatly contributing to the material development of that portion of the State, will add to the business interests of Alexandia, which is the natural market for all that section of country.

THE ALEXANDRIA AND WASHINGTON RAIL ROAD

Is a valuable link between the cities of Alexandria and Washington, six miles in length, by which these cities are brought into close and frequent communication. At one mile and a half from Alexandria, the Washington and Ohio Rail Road has formed a connection with this road, and over it its passengers and freight, for Washington City and points north and west, pass daily without change of cars. The Baltimore and Potomac Rail Road Company has very recently completed, and now uses, a substantial railroad bridge, one mile in length, which spans the Potomac at Washington.

THE ALEXANDRIA CANAL

Is seven miles long, and extends from the terminus of the Chesapeake and Ohio Canal at Georgetown, D. C., to Alexandria. It crosses the Potomac River at Georgetown by means of a magnificent aqueduct, and, in connection with the Chesapeake and Ohio Canal, is largely engaged in the transportation of coal from Cumberland, Md. The fine facilities afforded at Alexandria, for its storage and shipment, enable this city to enjoy a liberal share of this important trade, as is shown by the coal at the wharves, and the shipping taking in freight.

The high price of coal in England has recently developed a new trade in the shipment, from Alexandria direct to Aspinwall and San Francisco, of large supplies of Cumberland coal for the use of the steam lines engaged in the China and Japan seas ; and in case these prices are maintained, it is reasonable to suppose that, in a short time, the ports of the West Indies, Central and South America will be supplied, in a great degree, by shipment from Alexandria.

MANUFACTURES.

Alexandria presents great advantages as a location for manufacturing establishments of all kinds.

The low price of city property, and the great demand for manufactured articles, offer inducements to men of capital and enterprise to establish tanneries, iron foundries, shoe factories, machine shops, paper mills, breweries; factories for making agricultural implements, buckets,' tubs, brooms, barrels, matches, etc.; railroad car works; fertilizer and cement mills; stove foundries; tobacco, woollen, and cotton factories ; and, in short, every branch of mechanical industry would prosper in the hands of enterprising men with capital.

It has now in successful operation one steam cotton factory employing 125 operatives; two iron foundries and machine shops ; three coach factories; two steam planing mills and sash factories ; one extensive tannery, the largest in the State, with a branch in the interior; two steam breweries, one very extensive ; two brick works, one ope-

3

rated by steam ; two lime-kilns, which fail to supply the demand ; one pottery; two extensive steam sumac mills; one ship yard, operated on a limited scale; an additional one, with liberal capital and energetically conducted, would meet with good success ; one establishment for the manufacture of mineral waters, and four furniture manufactories, in addition to numerous other branches of industry. It has two daily newspapers, two tri-weekly, and four weekly.

The machine shops and locomotive and car works of the Orange, Alexandria, and Manassas, and the Washington and Ohio Rail Roads, at Alexandria, are very extensive and complete. These works give employment to a large number of mechanics and artisans, and the work they turn out will compare favorably with that of similar establishments in the country. The Potomac fisheries (long noted for their value), and the Chesapeake oyster trade, afford employment to a very considerable portion of the population of Alexandria.

The educational advantages of Alexandria are well known. It has excellent male and female seminaries and schools. Its public schools are not excelled by any similar institutions in the country. The whole number of graded public schools during the year ending August 31, 1872, was 6 ; number of teachers, 16 ; number of pupils, 983, of which there were 612 white, and 371 colored; total cost of education, $9884 72. At the same time there were 32 private and parochial schools, with 1255 pupils, of which there were of white children 933, and 322 colored. There were fully 85 per cent. of the white, and 70 per cent. of the colored children between the ages of six and sixteen at school last year.

Alexandria has twenty churches of various denominations, all of which are generally well supported.

With all these and the other advantages it is known to possess, it is not too much to say that Alexandria is growing in wealth and importance, and offers a fine field to enterprising men of capital from the other sections of the country and from Europe.

ALEXANDRIA COUNTY, VA.

This county embraces a small extent of territory on the west side of the Potomac River, north of the city of Alexandria, and south and opposite to the cities of Washington and Georgetown. Its greatest length is about ten miles, and its width about four miles. Exclusive of the city of Alexandria, the seat of justice, which is embraced within the limits of the county, the population in 1870 was 3185.

The great railway lines, between the North and South, pass through this county a distance of six miles, and the Washington and Ohio Rail Road traverses it, in a northwest direction, a distance of about eight miles.

It has two good turnpikes, several county roads, and three splendid bridges (over the Potomac) leading to the District cities. Two of these bridges are *free*, and are kept in order by the United States government. These advantages, together with its proximity to the markets of Alexandria, Washington, and Georgetown, render the lands in this county very valuable as truck farms or market gardens, these cities affording a demand for all the crops that are produced.

Within the past six years extensive brick works have been put in operation on the lands in this county contiguous to what is known as the LONG BRIDGE, and supply, in a great measure, the material used in the great improvements now being prosecuted in the city of Washington. These enterprises have increased the population of the county fully 2000 since last census (1870), when it was reported at 3185.

The Arlington estate, the seat of the late George Washington Parke Custis, and of his son-in-law, the late General Robert E. Lee, is in this county, on the hills overlooking the city of Washington, three miles distant. This splendid domain, embracing over one thousand acres of land, is now the property of the United States government, and is used as a National Cemetery for the burial of the soldiers of the Union who fell in the late terrible conflict between the States of the North and South, and as such is an object of great interest to visitors from this and other lands.

In Alexandria county there are eight public schools with nine teachers, having 423 pupils, 197 white and 226 colored, the whole costing $3247 65. Sixty-one per cent. of all persons between the ages of five and twenty-one years attended school during the year ending August 31, 1872.

FAIRFAX COUNTY, VA.

The Potomac River and the county of Alexandria bound it on the east, the county of Loudoun lies on the west, and Prince William county on the west and south. It is drained by the Potomac River, the Occoquan River, and their tributaries.

The Orange, Alexandria, and Manassas Rail Road passes through this county in a westerly direction, the Alexandria and Fredericksburg Rail Road through its southeastern, and the Washington and Ohio Rail Road along its northeastern border.

The surface is diversified with hills and level lands. The soil, when properly cultivated, is very productive, and much of the neglected land has been, and is now being, reclaimed and put under a more thorough system of culture and proves to be highly productive.

Within the past few years this county has had the benefit of a considerable immigration from the Northern and Western States, and from England, and as a consequence has undergone material improvement in the better tillage of the lands. Many new buildings have been erected, new farms opened, and miles of new fencing inclose fertile fields which the late war caused the owners to abandon.

The population of the county in 1870 was 12,952, an increase over that of 1860, notwithstanding the late war, and its effects on its prosperity.

Fairfax C. H., the county seat, fifteen miles from Alexandria and Washington, lies between the Orange, Alexandria, and Manassas Rail Road and the Washington and Ohio Rail Road, three and a half miles from the former, at Fairfax Station, and four and a half miles from Vienna, a thrifty village and station, on the latter. Its location is elevated, very healthy, with the purest atmosphere and water, and is surrounded with a lovely panorama. Here are located the usual county buildings where WASHINGTON had often appeared, and where his original will is preserved. The population of the Court House is 500 or 600.

MOUNT VERNON, in life the home of the great Washington, and now his resting-place, is situated on the Potomac, ten miles below Alexandria, in Fairfax county, is kept in fine state of preservation, and by steamer is frequented daily by many visitors, foreign as well as native, and is also accessible by a good road from Alexandria.

THE THEOLOGICAL SEMINARY of Virginia is in this county. This institution, in a properly organized form, was opened in Alexandria in 1823. In 1827, after the erection of the first building, it was removed to its present site, a hill 250 feet above the level of the Potomac, two and a half miles west of Alexandria, and seven miles in a direct line from Washington, overlooking both cities and the river. In February, 1854, a charter was granted by the Legislature of Virginia, and soon afterwards new buildings were erected. These consist of the Library, St. George's Hall, Aspinwall Hall, Bohlen Hall, and Meade Hall. The buildings, besides these, are the Professors' houses and the Chapel. Within a few hundred yards of the Seminary is the Diocesan High School. The legal style of the corporation is " The Protestant Episcopal Theological Seminary and High School in Virginia." The post-office address is " Theological Seminary, Fairfax County, Virginia."

The Washington and Ohio Rail Road enters Fairfax County eight miles from Alexandria, and, in a northwest direction, passes through it a distance of about twenty miles. It has five stations in this county, viz.: Falls Church, Vienna, Hunter's Mill, Thornton, and Herndon.

Falls Church, an old settlement, takes its name from the "Great Falls" of the Potomac, a few miles distant. The village still contains its earliest "settler," in the shape of a venerable but well-preserved brick edifice, known as Falls Church. This building is held in great veneration by the people; the material used in its construction was imported from England prior to the Revolution; since then it has passed through three foreign wars, and one *slight* "home unpleasantness."

Falls Church is in the township of that name, which contains 2461 inhabitants; is on the Leesburg, Alexandria, and Washington Turnpike; is seven miles from the county seat, and by the Washington and Ohio Rail Road ten miles from Alexandria and Washington.

Within the past few years this village and the adjacent country show marked improvement. Many new buildings of modern style have been erected, and immigration and the improved tillage of the soil contribute to the general prosperity. Many officers and employés of the government, stationed at Washington, reside in this vicinity, and pass daily to and from Washington over the railroad. An extensive nursery is located at Falls Church, and during the past year the freight and passenger business of the Washington and Ohio Rail Road, at this station, has increased fully one hundred per cent. over the preceding year.

Vienna Station is in Providence township, five miles west of Falls Church, and fifteen from Alexandria and Washington—a new village, and one of the fruits of the railroad; it contains about 150 inhabitants. In this vicinity the land is equal to any on the railroad east of Goose Creek. The village contains about twenty houses, three stores, one plow foundry doing a good business, a grist and saw mill, blacksmith, wagon and harness makers' establishments, churches, and a new public school-house having fifty scholars.

The Newtown, Bucks County (Pennsylvania) *Enterprise*, in a late number, says: "Doctor B. M. Collins, formerly of Bucks County, Pennsylvania, now residing on his farm, near Vienna Station, writes, that his farming operations have succeeded beyond his expectations. It is not a land flowing with milk and honey, but the soil is easily worked and more quickly renovated by lime and manure than Bucks

County land. Being only fourteen miles from Washington and Alexandria, these fertilizers are cheap and abundant. He gets lime at Vienna Station, on Washington and Ohio Rail Road, two miles from his farm.

"The Doctor has named his place ‘Pleasant View,’ and it is a most agreeable home—good society, and much better climate than here. The air south of the Potomac range of hills is unusually bland and free, even in mid-winter, from sharp, long-continued freezing keenness, enabling them to commence work very early in the spring, and to continue often till New Year's.

"Labor is abundant at moderate prices, and quick sale for every kind of produce at Washington, and but one day required to attend market and return.

"Buyers of land are steadily coming in, and about thirty deeds are recorded at the court-house every month. Good farms, with necessary buildings, bring about $30 per acre. It cannot be many years before land so advantageously situated, with its unusual market facilities and salubrious climate, will rival the best Pennsylvania farms in value.

"Fairfax has three railroads, crossing the county about ten miles apart, and two more in prospect. From about fifteen stations passengers can take the cars daily and go to any part of the United States. With so many advantages to recommend it, the Doctor advises all persons who think of changing location to come and examine the many excellent farms for sale in Fairfax and the adjoining counties."

HUNTER'S MILL STATION is three miles west of Vienna, and eighteen from Alexandria and Washington. Apart from the postal facilities afforded at this station, this place is of but little importance. The people of this neighborhood use Vienna Station as their depot for receiving supplies and shipping their productions.

THORNTON STATION, twenty-one miles from Alexandria, is located in a thickly wooded country, which supplies vast quantities of railroad ties, rails for fencing, fire-wood, and timber. Within the past three years two cargoes of ship timber for the French market were cut and shipped from this depot to Havre, via the Washington and Ohio Rail Road to Alexandria.

Three miles north from Thornton's is the village of Drainsville, the country surrounding which supplies business to the railroad to some

extent, but, lying upon a good turnpike leading to Alexandria, Washington, and Georgetown, the people of that portion of the county
generally find it more convenient to use the turnpike in the transportation of their products to market. The lands in this neighborhood,
convenient to the station, were purchased a few years ago by an
English gentleman, who has expended a considerable sum of money
in the development of this portion of the country.

HERNDON STATION, twenty-three miles from Alexandria, is an important point on the Washington and Ohio Rail Road. Within a comparatively short period a considerable number of thrifty farmers have
settled in this vicinity from the Northern and Western States. It has
the advantage of a good supply of fine timber lying within easy
reach of the depot. This is being converted into hogshead shook,
which are shipped to Cuba with profit to the manufacturer. A large
operator in this material, from the State of Maine, recently made a
heavy purchase of timbered lands three miles from the depot; and the
low price at which these lands were purchased enables him to place
the manufactured article in Cuba at a less figure than those engaged
in the same trade in Baltimore and other northern cities.

Besides the heavy shipments of fire-wood from this station to Alexandria and Washington, the supply necessary for the use of the Washington and Ohio Rail Road is considerable, and affords a ready
market for all that is offered. Herndon is the shipping point for the
neighboring villages of Dranesville, Chantilly, Spring Vale, and
Frying Pan.

A paper prepared by H. C. Williams, Esq., on fruit culture, and
the inducements to engage in this branch of rural industry throughout the country he has sketched, is here introduced.

Major Williams is a native of the State of Georgia, and was an intelligent planter in the State of Tennessee. After many years' ser-
vice under the government of the United States he retired to a farm
near Vienna Station, Fairfax County, on which he had previously
planted extensive orchards, since which time (1850) he has been a
devoted fruit-grower. Believing that he understood the subject in all
its bearings, and wishing to present reliable information thereon, a
contribution on this subject was solicited from him, to which attention is here invited:—

DESCRIPTIVE SKETCH OF THE COUNTRY FROM ALEXANDRIA TO THE BLUE RIDGE—MINERALS—SOILS—ADAPTABILITY TO GARDENING AND FRUIT CULTURE.

I NOW proceed to comply with your request to furnish some notes on the geological features of the section of country traversed by the Washington and Ohio Rail Road, between Alexandria and the Blue Ridge, with the minerals that occur in the several formations; also, the soils derived from the rocky strata, and their influence in fruit culture. Strictly speaking, this would confine me to the counties of Fairfax and Loudoun; but in the general way in which I purpose to treat the subjects before me, my remarks will be found applicable to all the northern counties embraced in what is popularly called the Piedmont region of Virginia.

If a line were drawn across the State from any point on tide-water to the western border, the same geological formations would be passed over. It is, however, proper to observe that the tertiary formations in the southern part of the State cover a large area, while north of Fredericksburg they are scarcely developed. Therefore, on the line of the road, as soon as we reach the first terrace or secondary banks of the Potomac, we are on rocks of the primordial series. These rocks are seen at Arlington Old Mills, and Carlin's Springs, and are a prolongation of the strata which cross the Potomac between the Little Falls and Georgetown.

Near the eighth mile-post on the road we enter upon another series of rocks overlying those we have passed. These rocks are talcose slates and schists, which crumble down readily, forming a soil of peculiar characteristics. The direction of the strata has a general parallelism with the Blue Ridge, and an average breadth of fifteen miles. This belt, for convenience sake, will be called in this paper the *Talcose schist formation.* It extends to Herndon, and has an average breadth of fifteen miles.

The soil formed by the disintegrated schists has a loose texture; is unctuous to the touch; is light, in the usual meaning of the term; and warm. It varies in color in proportion to the iron contained in the rocks, and its different states of oxidation. It parts freely with water, and, where the surface drainage is good, which is seldom otherwise, there is the required "bottom heat," an object never out of view with professional horticulturists.

There are but few minerals occurring in this formation. *Talc and soapstone* are found in some parts of Fairfax County. *Kaolin* or *porcelain clay* is abundant. It is first seen in the ridge below Falls

Church, near the eastern outcrop of this formation. East of Vienna there are several beds of more or less thickness, alternating with the layers of schists, and extending along the road for nearly the eighth of a mile. The greater portion of the *kaolin* is a pure white; it is in a state of great fineness, and may contain a very small percentage of talc. Submitting specimens to Dr. Antisell, while chief chemist to the U. S. Agricultural Department, he gave it as his opinion that it would be of great value in forming a glaze for the higher class of porcelain ware. This substance, not being required for any purpose in a country where agriculture is nearly the only pursuit of the inhabitants, has so far remained unused and unnoticed; but its locality being within half a mile of a railway station and flourishing village, it cannot be supposed that it will much longer be unappropriated. A plentiful, healthful country, with a good site for buildings for manufactories, on a railroad, fourteen and a half miles from a commercial city, with hourly trains to the national metropolis, wood and water convenient and abundant, with such advantages as a mineral of such value, should invite enterprise and capital.

The next change in geological features takes place near Herndon. It. is a trap-ridge, and, beyond yielding some basalts and minerals usual to such intrusions, possesses but little interest. It however appears to mark the eastern boundary of the next-named formation.

The *Triassic* or *Red Sandstone formation* spreads out from the ridge just passed to the foot of Catoctin Mountain, a distance of about twenty miles. Here the rocks of the Blue Ridge system first appear, and, having a dip to the south, a synclinal valley is formed, along which the calcareous breccia, or " Potomac marble" of former days, is strewn in large masses. This material, once so popular for architectural purposes, is, by the discovery of other marbles, now only valuable for being converted into lime.

The *Red Sandstone* is one of the most durable building stones in the country. The Smithsonian Institution in Washington is built of it. On the line of the road it is often seen in layers of different thickness, easily separable, and should the demand in the city continue, the quarrying and sending it there will doubtless at no distant day be a profitable business.

The disintegration of this sandstone forms a dark or reddish-brown soil. It is open and porous, and, like all soils in which silex preponderates, admits the free sinking of water. Having less capillary attraction than clayey soils, where deep tillage has been practised, droughts rarely injure growing crops.

In this formation few minerals have been discovered. Some years since there were a number of beds of the *sulphate of baryta* scattered through the counties of Fauquier and Prince William, but they have been exhausted. Traces of copper are found in some of the layers of this formation, but are not to be regarded as indications of any valuable deposit.

The next formation as we ascend the country west of Leesburg is composed of the various rocks peculiar to the Blue Ridge. These consist of gneiss, clayslate, hornblende, greenstone, quartz, mica, talcose schists, epidote, and chlorite. The rocks appear in great confusion, in consequence of the pitching and folding of the strata during the upheaval of the Blue Ridge and its outlines. As a consequence of such violent action and subsequent denudation and disintegration of the various rocks, the Piedmont region is eminently diversified by its minor ridges, numerous foot hills, gentle undulations, and level plains.

A soil derived from the disintegration of so many kinds of rocks, rich in the elements of vegetable nutrition, would at once establish its claims to a high reputation for fertility. The undecomposed rocks yet on the surface or slightly imbedded, containing lime, potash, and the oxides of iron, constitute a reserve in the soil which annual crops will not exhaust for ages. The crumbling down of the gneissoidal rocks in this section leaves on the surface small whitish pebbles, forming what are locally called "hominy soils." These pebbles contain at least twelve per cent. of potash. The potash is liberated slowly by atmospheric agencies, and, being washed down the sides of the hills, shows its effects in a luxurious vegetation. The small barren knolls, instead of being waste places on the farm, are really its supporters of fertility. The soil also contains lime, magnesia, and the oxides of iron, and is capable of growing a great variety of plants. The coarse particles of which the soil is composed prevent washing, which is eminently suggestive of deep tillage. Every farmer who plows deep one year is but bringing up matters to be pulverized and form fertilizing ingredients for his next year's crop.*

Although the great source of wealth in the Piedmont range consists in its multiplied agricultural capabilities, it is not destitute of valuable

* These remarks will be better understood by the following quotation from Baron Liebig : "A thousandth part of loam mixed with the quartz in the new red sandstone (Triassic), or with the lime in the different limestone formations, affords as much potash to the soil only twenty inches in depth as is sufficient to supply a forest of pines growing upon it for a century. A single cubit of feldspar is sufficient to supply a wood covering a surface of 26,910 square feet with the potash required for five years."

minerals. The calcareous breccia has been already mentioned. A quarry of marble is now being opened on the lands of Mr. Carter, on Goose Creek, in Loudoun County. Its texture and purity adapt it to the highest purposes of statuary. Crystallized marble of excellent quality occurs on the lands of Mr. George S. Ayre, near Upperville. On Dr. A. S. Payne's farm, near Markham station, in Fauquier County, marble again appears, the outcrops forming large ridges and hills, indicating an inexhaustible deposit. It is penetrated by crystals of epidote, and contains other mineral matters often disseminated as a coloring, which give to polished specimens a beauty and variegation equal to any other marble in the world.

As a building stone where a smooth surface is not desirable, the quartzite slates at Thoroughfare Gap cannot be excelled for strength or durability. The layers are of thicknesses from a few inches to a foot or more. These can be taken out of the strata of any desired length and breadth, and are as smooth on the sides as if they had passed through a mill.

Years ago a bed of iron ore was worked at the foot of the Catoctin Mountain, near the Point of Rocks on the Potomac. Indications of the existence of iron are frequent along the base of that mountain.

Asbestos has been discovered in Loudoun County. Ochres are abundant in the Piedmont range.

GENERAL FEATURES OF THE COUNTRY.

The country rises from tide water to the Blue Ridge, the summit of which by the railroad surveys has an altitude of one thousand and eighty-four feet. The surface is rolling; gentle declivities affording ample means for surface drainage. Small streams abound, and springs of purest water are on nearly every farm. When necessary to sink wells, water equal to that of the springs is procured at a depth seldom beyond the lifting power of the common pump. There are no marshes or stagnant pools to cause malarious diseases.

Forests of the original growth are yet interspersed through the country. In many places a growth of young pines shows that the lands have become partially deteriorated by continued cropping, and have been turned out to rest and recuperate by a natural process. After sustaining a forest of pines for about twenty years, oaks and hickories begin to appear, proving that the lands are again becoming fitted for the plow. This course of exhaustion and renovation has sometimes been censured by superficial critics, yet it has its beneficial effects. It preserves a just balance in heat and moisture, keeps the country supplied with wood, shelters growing crops from strong winds, and preserves the health of the country.

As we ascend the country complaints are less frequent in regard to losses by late spring and early autumn frosts. This is verified by my experience of thirty years as an orchardist. Though but four hundred and forty feet above the level of tide, it is a very rare occurrence to lose a crop of fruit by late spring frosts. On some of the elevations of the Piedmont region aged persons are to be found who will say that they never knew the fruit to be destroyed by late spring frosts. Perhaps their memories may be sometimes at fault, but after being an observer of meteorological phenomena for the Smithsonian Institution for some years past, and reviewing the observations of my son for the same purpose made on the eastern slope of the Blue Ridge, at an elevation of about nine hundred feet, I must say that the disasters from this cause are as unfrequent as in any other part of the United States.

With this brief preliminary sketch I will now endeavor to give the fruit-growing capabilities of the country, and incidentally to state the inducements to increased culture.

SMALL FRUITS AND GARDENING.

The lands adjacent to the railroad are well adapted to the cultivation of all the small fruits and vegetables peculiar to the climate. The strawberry, raspberry, and blackberry are indigenous plants. The latter when cultivated attains a large size and high flavor. If any of the varieties on the nurserymen's catalogues possess any merit over our wild variety when cultivated, I have not been able to discover it. Large quantities are annually gathered from the old fields and woods and sold in the Washington market. Other wild fruits are held in high esteem, and are sold at good prices ; whortleberries, chinquepins, chestnuts, walnuts, and hickory nuts may be mentioned as always being in demand.

Large fields of strawberries are cultivated, and yet the supply falls short of the demand. Raspberries, gooseberries, and currants have an increasing demand ; indeed, of these small fruits it may be correctly said that the public appetite "grows by what it feeds upon."

In garden vegetables, everything required for the most sumptuous tables is grown to perfection. Here, as in other cases, to enable persons not acquainted with the productions of our soil and climate, I will mention the following vegetables grown by the most simple means of cultivation : Peas, beans, potatoes (both Irish and sweet), watermelons, canteloupes, pumpkins, squashes, cucumbers, cabbages, turnips, radishes, asparagus, spinach, celery, tomatoes, peanuts (Arachishypogea), leeks, and onions.

For raising poultry, this is excelled by no other country.

For truck farms, or large gardens devoted to the cultivation of vegetables to supply the city markets, the lands adjacent to the railroads are admirably adapted. The undulating surface of the country gives every desired exposure; the higher grounds being warm and dry, and the intervales retentive of moisture, and cool, the skilful gardener can be at no loss for the proper location of his plants. It may be said, also, that effective modes of irrigation might be introduced at a moderate expense. The great accession to the population of the city of Washington within the last ten years, without a corresponding increase in the several classes of producers, has led to high prices in the vegetable market, and caused the supply to be drawn from a distance. It cannot be supposed that such a state of things will become permanent, for high prices are too great incentives to production to permit it to become so. A change has already begun, and the increased railway facilities will have the effect of reducing the expenses of market gardening. Heretofore this business was followed only by persons in the vicinity of the city, who used their own means of transportation. Relatively their numbers have not increased, and the necessary supply must reach the city by railroads. The cheap lands adjacent to the railroad offer superior inducements in this direction.

Since my first acquaintance in the city of Washington, market gardening has been a lucrative business, and I could mention the names of many persons who have acquired handsome fortunes by following it.

Since the restoration of peace the following villages have sprung up, being one of the first results of the successful operation of the Washington and Ohio Rail Road: Vienna, Herndon, Guilford, Farmwell, and Clark's Gap, all of which have become business centres of neighborhood industries. At these places country produce meets a ready sale to persons engaged in a traffic between the city and country. Literally, a farmer or a gardener may have a market at his own door.

The cheapness of living and the proverbial health of the country have induced a number of mechanics to settle in the villages to follow their vocations. Of one only I shall speak. At Vienna, where at the close of the war there were only a few half-destroyed houses, and one family residing, there are now three stores, two wheelwright shops, two blacksmiths' shops, a steam saw and grist mill, a chair-maker's shop (about to be established), a foundry and plow manufactory. As an instance that mechanical pursuits can be followed successfully in the country, I will state that during the present year a large order for wagons was filled in Vienna for persons in business in Washington City.

The attractions of the country, with its healthfulness and cheapness of living, now that these are opened by railway conveniences, are beginning to be appreciated by officers of the public departments in Washington City. A number of these have their residences near the stations, going to and returning daily from their places of business at a less annual expense than forty years ago they could have reached their offices and returned home had they resided in Georgetown, not two miles distant. A public officer in Washington, with a salary of $2000 per annum, may expect to pay $500 for a house, or $2000 in four years. If living in the country, and going to and returning on an annual ticket, for $60 per annum for four years, or $240, there would be a saving in the item of house rent alone of $1760, a sum sufficient to pay for a small tract of land and erect a comfortable cottage on it.

In other respects, the saving that could be effected by keeping one or two cows, raising poultry, growing garden vegetables and fruits, if for private use only, the expense of supporting a family would be reduced to a nominal sum.

FRUIT GROWING.

With the preceding excursive remarks, I will now proceed to the consideration of fruit culture. How far the foregoing may be regarded as necessary and proper to a correct understanding of the subject, it is not my province to judge. But if it should be charged that I have spent too much time in elucidating irrelevant matters, and prolixity of style, I can but say in my defence that I did so to present the matter in all its bearings, to enable persons not having a personal knowledge of the country to form proper conclusions. They can determine when and how far it can be connected with other pursuits, or whether to engage in this business alone.

Virginians engaged in agricultural pursuits, like most other people, have given their attention to the cultivation of those staples which entered into the commerce of the country. Until late years, there being no home market for fruit, farmers contented themselves with growing only such as were required for family use. In the progress of the age this thing has passed away. Now, by the growth of our neighboring city of Washington, we have a demand in excess over production, with the assurance which quick and safe transportation give, that when we shall be able to produce a surplus over home consumption it can be disposed of in distant markets at remunerative prices.

Every experienced pomologist who has travelled through Virginia has been favorably impressed with the fruit-growing capabilities of the State. Such was the opinion generally expressed by the members of the American Pomological Society, which held its last biennial meeting in Richmond, the State capital, in September, 1871. That meeting was attended by delegates and members from every State and territory in the Union, with few exceptions. Though this State was but partially represented in the exhibition of fruits, it was a subject of general remark that in the quality and variety of our peaches, apples, pears, quinces, plums, grapes, and figs no other State in the Union could compete with us.

The Potomac Fruit Growers' Association, composed mostly of citizens from other States who have settled in the vicinity of Washington in years past, held its first annual meeting in that city in last September. The display of fruits on that occasion, the first for nineteen years, was such as to excite the wonder and astonishment of all experienced and scientific pomologists present. The collection of grapes and pears was pronounced by Mr. John Saul, whose name carries authority with it on such subjects, to be the largest in variety and best in quality that had ever been exhibited in the United States. There were also fine assortments of peaches and apples for the season. In the course of the discussion, a member, formerly a citizen of New York, stated the exalted opinion of Mr. Charles Downing in regard to fruit culture in this State.

After stating opinions of such high authority, it may be thought that I should rest the case. I should do so if I were addressing pomologists, who have an opportunity to investigate the peculiarities of our soil. But having had thirty years' experience in fruit culture in this locality, and within the last five years having assisted in planting trees and vines on the red-sandstone formation, and in the Piedmont region, I will devote the remainder of this article to the discussion of the varieties proper to be planted, some of the results I have attained, and probably better success that yet awaits those who will engage in this interesting department of rural industry.

1. *Of the Apple.*

When selections have been judiciously made, every part of the State has produced this fruit in perfection. I shall confine my remarks to the district herein sketched. My original selection was made with the best lights before me thirty years ago. It should be borne in mind that was about the time that fruit culture in the Northern States was attracting increased attention, but it did not assume a definite shape until the great work of the late A. J. Downing, published in 1845, gave method and science to an art variously practised. My object was to make an orchard in the first place to supply my family, and send the remainder to market. I endeavored to secure a succession from the earliest summer to the latest winter-keeping varieties. The selection was good, and has been improved by other sorts as they have since risen into favor. The first planting was in the spring of 1843, but additions were made for several years afterwards. The location was on a farm through which the Washington and Ohio Rail Road now runs, one mile from the village of Vienna. The elevation is four hundred and forty-five feet above the level of tide-water.

Residing in Washington at the time, I was under the necessity of trusting the management of the trees to persons not accustomed to the management of orchards. It was not until 1853 that the trees gave a good crop, and that year, at the first fair of the Virginia State Agricultural Society, I was awarded the premium " for the largest and best variety of apples adapted to general cultivation in the State."

The following varieties I can confidently recommend for cultivation in the districts before noticed as the *Talcose slate* and *Triassic* formations.

Summer Varieties.—Red Astrachan, Early Bough, Yellow Harvest, Porter, Gravestein, Red-streak, Hagloe, Summer Queen. Maiden's Blush. To these may be added Edward's Early, a very promising new sort.

Fall Varieties.—Wetherell's White Sweet, Tulpehocken, Benoni, Rambo, Fall Harvey, Fall Pippin.

Late Fall and Early Winter.—Wine, Bullock's Pippin, Roman Stem, Smokehouse and Hix's White.

Mid Winter.—Smith's Cider, Genet, Winesap, Pomme d'Api or Lady Apple.

Late Winter and Spring.—Tewksbury, American Pippin or Grindstone, late Russet.

Few persons who make orchards for profit would be willing to plant all these varieties. All are of the highest merit, and I give the list more to be a guide to the best varieties of their season than as recommending them for a single orchard. Summer varieties are seldom profitable, for the reason that peaches and pears, which ripen with them, are preferred for the dessert. For drying every orchard should have a few of the higher flavored sorts.

The following varieties (mostly of southern origin) deserve extensive trial, and are recommended to those who are fond of experimenting and testing the merits of fruits, viz : Limber-twig, Ben Davis, Equinately, Hall's Red, Meade's Kuper, Milan, Nickijack, Shockley, Mattamuskeet, and Cannon Pearmain. Experiments, however, had better be left to nurserymen, and after the orchards are made of the most popular varieties at the time, additions can be introduced from those which give most promise. For market the following fall and winter varieties meet the readiest sales : Rambo, Smokehouse, Bullock's Pippin, Smith's Cider, Genet, Winesap, Pomme d'Api, and Tewksbury. These will give a succession from the first killing frost in autumn till the following June.

All the varieties named in the first list succeed well on the soils derived from the metamorphic rocks of the Piedmont region. There, however, it would be well to substitute the Milan, London Pippin, and the Albemarle Pippin, for the Roman Stem, American Pippin, and Late Russet.

For the New York market and for shipment to England, the Pomme d'Api and Albemarle Pippin command the highest prices. By the *New York Tribune* of November 16th, 1872, the Pomme d'Api is quoted at from $6 to $9 per barrel, while $3 is the highest price offered for other varieties. It here keeps well till February, and then is in perfection, but, unfortunately, its great beauty and attractiveness cause it to be sacrificed long before it should be used for the dessert.

An erroneous opinion prevails in regard to the time required for a young orchard to come into bearing. It is usually stated to be ten years. In that time I am confident that I could make an orchard with trees two years old from the graft pay all expenses, and for the land they stood on if not held at an extravagant figure. I know that this will be considered a bold assertion. But I am certain that, when my practice shall be tested by well-established principles of vegetable physiology, I shall be acquitted of any charge derogatory to the character of a veteran orchardist. I have made known my mode of training young trees to but a small circle of friends, and insisted that they should satisfy themselves whether there was any humbug or necromancy in it. This opportunity enables me to give my theories a wider range, and I do so for the purpose of inducing others to engage in fruit culture to augment their own wealth and benefit mankind.

In the first place, if I have a well-grown stocky tree two years from the graft, I head it back to the lowest well-developed buds, of course,

4

on the previous year's growth ; I shall omit all other things in regard to setting the tree, supposing they will be properly done, and only give what may be regarded as new in practice. The object in view is to start two branches near the ground, say between two and three feet. The young tree is to be watched, and the whole of the vital forces thrown into the two branches, stopping the growth of all other shoots. Some trees will make a vigorous growth the first year, but it is better to take two years in forming the next bifurcation than to do so in one. The following season the two branches are to be shortened back about four feet from the ground. On each of these branches another bifurcation is to be formed in the manner of the preceding year. There are now four limbs to constitute the framework of the future tree, which will require little pruning for several years. The fourth year after planting it will usually begin to bear fruit, and as the roots are well established before it has much head, it will soon make up lost time, and continue to grow and bear fruit. Low heads are required in this climate, and short stems always make the most healthy trees. The several deflections of the sap from a vertical line promote the ripening of the wood and the early formation of fruit buds. In this climate trees in good soils are inclined to run too much to wood, and I plant trees for fruit, not to grow timber. I shall follow this practice until I quit the business.

Another very good way is to head back, and let three buds push to form the future head. The other mode is preferable.

This article being intended for the information of emigrants, it is an object with me to give such details as will enable such as desire to form orchards to do so at once. There are several large nursery establishments in the State, conducted by gentlemen of probity and intelligence, from whom all the desired nursery stock can be obtained on favorable terms, and strangers will find it to their interest to patronize them.

Before leaving the subject of the apple, it is but proper to observe that it is the opinion of many distinguished pomologists that the belt of country which in this as well as in general use is called the " Piedmont region," embracing the outline and numerous foot-hills of the Blue Ridge, constitute the best apple-growing district in the United States. The special recommendations are, first, the elevation and consequent exemption from loss of crops by late frosts in spring, which both meteorological data and experience confirm; and, secondly, by the decomposition of the metamorphic rocks, which put lime and potash in the soil—mineral elements necessary to insure full development. Trees planted even in soils where the surface has been exhausted by superficial tillage, will grow and flourish for nearly a century. This is seen on many farms in this region, where old trees have stood, " whereof the memory of man runneth not to the contrary." Shipments of apples have already been made from this part of the State to England, where they command the highest price. While I fully accord with the opinions of the pomologists from other States. as before stated, with the reasons for my concurrence, I must say that it is so easy a matter to prepare the soil for trees by composts, that persons not living within this highly-favored region need not despair of successfully growing the apple.

2. *The Pear and Quince.*

The same soil which is required for the apple is also required for the pear. Here it succeeds to perfection. For varieties no other part of the United States is more celebrated, and probably there is not any other place more highly favored by exemption from the blight. I have cultivated the pear since 1845; the Bloodgood. the Bartlett, Beurré Diel, Flemish Beauty, Urbaniste, Seckel, and Winter Nelis; and none of these have shown any signs of that much-dreaded disease. Other cultivators have introduced new varieties, and have been rewarded to their entire satisfaction. This can but prove to be one of our most remunerative fruits, whether grown on dwarfs or standards.

The quince, also, attains fine size, and would doubtless be a profitable fruit if grown for the New York market, where it is always in demand.

3. *The Peach.*

This has been 'the fruit *par excellence* of the Washington market. and, before the war, was grown in immense quantities. During that unfortunate period many fine orchards were destroyed, and no new ones were planted. For several years past there has been a comparative scarcity, and the supply had to be brought from a distance. But the orchards are now coming into bearing, and their fruit will have the preference for its superior size and freshness.

On our talcose, warm soils it attains the highest perfection. I have had specimens to weigh eleven and a half ounces, and equal in flavor to any I have eaten, grown in the States of Tennessee, Arkansas, and Texas. It is in season from the 25th of July to the 10th of October. or rather these are the extremes of the season for the best table varieties. The market for our home-raised sorts usually begins about the first of August. When properly cared for the fruit comes into

bearing very early. This year I sold some fruit from trees planted
one year from the bud in April, 1870. I raised the trees myself, and
several of my friends who planted from the same nursery had their
trees to come into bearing, as also my younger son, who has his orchard on the Blue Ridge slope. His trees were from the nursery of
Mr. John Saul, in Washington City. Our mode of training is to
shorten back the first two years, and after that time to pursue a sort
of shortening back and renewal system. Our object is to keep the
heads low, and not too much bearing wood. Notwithstanding all my
efforts to keep my trees low, some are now fifteen feet high, with twelve
feet diameter of head. I used no compost but wood ashes, and cultivated the orchard in potatoes, peas, and beans. The ground for the
potatoes was composted with sawdust and other vegetable matters,
with lime to decompose them, and the potatoes when prepared for
planting were whitened with ground gypsum. The largest specimen
of the crop of 1870 weighed in Alexandria one pound and twelve
ounces, last year about a pound and a quarter, and this year some
were again weighed in Alexandria, and notwithstanding the great
drought, one weighed one pound and three ounces. In all this
there is nothing extraordinary, though the newspapers in publishing
these facts considered it an unusual success; if so, it is as much
within the grasp of others as myself. The peach tree is not that
short-lived tree that it is further north. At the exhibition of fruits
by the Potomac Fruit Growers' Association I had peaches grown on
a tree twenty-seven years planted, and it looks good for ten more
crops. Here the disease called the "Yellows" which, as well as the
"Pear Blight," I maintain is caused by a defect in the soil in connection with atmospheric agencies, is wholly unknown. Trees are subject
to the attacks of the borer, but a little care at the proper time saves
loss. Here I will observe that neither this nor any other orchard
tree is ever killed by severe cold.

In the treassic or red sandstone belt the peach does equally well,
and the soil is admirably adapted to its cultivation. A stranger judg-
ing from the soil might give preference to the treassic, but having
had some experience on it also, I have only to say that with good
feeding with composts, in which wood-ashes constitute the basis, both
formations, as I have alluded to them, are equal.

Probably on the Blue Ridge slope, where the summer temperature
is slightly less than in the preceding, the peach may not by a shade
of difference be either as large or as finely flavored as in lower and
warmer regions, yet from specimens which I have seen there is much
to encourage its cultivation. It is now receiving increased attention.

Believing, however, that it will be a remunerative crop, I supplied my son, who has settled near Piedmont, in Fauquier County, with trees for an orchard, and so far they have given auspicious promises.

4. *Cherry.*

The last, though not the least, yet the most neglected of all of our orchard fruits, is the cherry. Not more than three or four good varieties have ever found their way into the Washington market, and not even in quantities sufficient to remove an ancient superstition that it is an unwholesome fruit. This prejudice was strengthened by the fact that the illness which brought on the death of President Taylor was caused by his having eaten some acid cherries and milk after an exposure for some hours to a hot fourth of July sun. A better ray of light is dispersing that darkness, and I find people ready to buy, eat, and preserve my Knight's Early Black, Black Tartarian, Grafflon and Downton Bigarreau, without effecting an insurance on their lives. So far as the question of health is concerned, I can say from an enlarged experience for one-third of my lifetime, that good ripe cherries are no more prejudicial to health than strawberries, luscious ripe peaches, or a Bartlett or a Seckel pear, and may be indulged in with the same impunity.

Throughout the whole line of the Washington and Ohio Rail Road, to which these remarks are applicable, the cherry flourishes in a higher state than in any other part of the United States with which I am acquainted. From seeds of the mazzards, introduced by the early settlers, trees have sprung up, often by the roadsides, which attain great age, and are so frequently interspersed among the indigenous growth that a person not acquainted with its history would never suspect it to be a wanderer from Asia. There can be no better proof of its adaptability to this section than the facts stated. I find these wildings to make excellent stocks for the better varieties. Thus propagated, the grafts grow freely and begin to bear fruit. This tree is often found growing among the young pines of the "abandoned lands," and really, from every indication, appears to prefer soils reduced by cultivation to fresh lands, provided that the location is on high, warm soils.

From my sales last season, though I did not send any to the Washington market, I feel warranted in recommending the extensive cultivation of this fruit. Even in the small villages of Vienna and Fairfax Court House, the demand at twelve and a half cents per quart was more than the supply. It was not convenient to send them to Washington, where double that price would have been given. The new process of "canning" has brought the cherry into great request; and, thus preserved, it is not only one of the most beautiful but one of the most delicious fruits for desserts. The facility of raising it, and certainty of the crops, will soon make its extensive multiplication one of the prominent features in Fairfax fruit culture. It will hold its superiority, for neither north nor south of this county can it be grown with equal success. Planters should not look to home market alone. We can, while the season lasts with us, take the lead in this fruit in the markets of Philadelphia and New York, and probably Boston.

With the cheap and safe fruit crate, a recent invention of Mr. E. B. Georgia, of Clifton in this county, which crate I have used with entire satisfaction, cherries can be sent by express from Alexandria to New York in less than ten hours, arriving there as fresh and as sound as when gathered from the tree.

5. *The Grape.*

This fruit, which of late years has attracted so much attention throughout the country, has not been neglected in this part of the State. It is now extensively grown for the Washington market. Before the late internecine disturbances a few vineyards had been commenced, and had begun to justify the reasonable expectations of the proprietors. Since the restoration of peace it was one of the branches of industry to which early attention was given, and numerous vineyards have been planted in the counties of Fairfax, Prince William, Loudoun, and Fauquier, while the extensive vineyards of M. B. Buck, Esq., in Warren County, in operation before the war, may be regarded as settling the question affirmatively that Virginia possesses unrivalled claims to pre-eminence. Even in this northern part we have all the climatic requirements of a wine-producing country. Nature has declared her purpose, but we have been slow in comprehending her lessons. On our low and moist lands, under the shade of forest trees, the Fox grape (*vitis labrasca*) flourishes with great vigor and productiveness. This is the parent of the Catawba, Isabella, Hartford Prolific, and the Concord, the most esteemed native sorts for table use. On the gentle rising grounds and stony knolls, with a full exposure to the sun, the summer grape (*vitis estivalis*) forms thickets, overpowering the undergrowth and giving most profuse crops of fruit. This species runs into innumerable sorts or subvarieties, of which the Clinton, Norton's Virginia, Herbemont, Alvey, Lenoir, and Devereux are the most celebrated. These are excellent table varieties, and from them, doubtless, the future wine grapes for the sections of country in which the Scuppernong will not succeed, are to be derived.

When the experiments of raising seedlings from these cultivated wild varieties shall have progressed as far as those which produced the Concord from a wild type, we may hope for as favorable results. In that case we can but have grapes that will form wines adapted to popular use.

My experience with the vine has been more that of a collector and experimenter with wild varieties than anything else. In 1857, under an engagement with the agricultural branch of the Patent Office, I visited the mountains in the State of Arkansas and the northern portion of Texas, to collect the native grapes which early explorers of those regions had so often eulogized in glowing terms. I returned, and the collection was placed in the hands of propagators. At the close of the year, when I was absent on another mission to Chihuahua, for the wine grape cultivated at El Paso, the original intention of the Department was changed from that of testing the merits of the grapes thus collected by the Department to that of scattering them broadcast over the country, where they came to nothing. A few in my private collection, however, escaped destruction during the war, and, after the few tests to which they have been subjected, I can truly say of them, in the language of Mr. George Hupman, the great Missouri vigneron: "They are dangerous rivals to the Norton's Virginia," which he considers a wine grape of highest merit. Of late years I have paid considerable attention to our home wild varieties, and have in my small collection hybrids between the Fox and summer varieties, as well as some summer sorts of which I entertain sanguine hopes. These facts should encourage us to give increased attention to vine culture. Virginia for this purpose furnishes, equal to any place I have explored, all the requirements of the vine, which appear to be a deep sandy soil, rich in potash, with a full sunny exposure. Such situations are found everywhere from tide water to the summit of the Blue Ridge. Our summer varieties are so little subject to blighting diseases, and are found to vary the quantity of their fruits with the season in so slight a degree, that the cultivator may rely with certainty upon the fruition of his hopes. Late spring frosts never do any injury to the vine, and our seasons are long enough to permit the thorough ripening of fruit and wood.

I do not feel myself called on to prove by statistics that vine culture has been remunerative to the proprietors of vineyards. Success in this, as well as in all other things, depends upon attention, industry, and good management. Yet, so far as my knowledge extends, no one is retiring in disgust, while every season of planting brings out hosts of new beginners. Information in vine culture is more sought from me than is asked in any other department of fruit culture.

Whether we shall ever succeed in making delicate, high-priced wines, is a problem, in my opinion, to be solved by chemistry. Our hopes for this end are very encouraging. We, already, by the simplest process form a cheap and wholesome beverage, which the more it is used will be the more popular. In social customs sudden revolutions are not to be expected, and it may be years before native wines will take the place of alcoholic drinks; but no revolution ever will take place unless a beginning is made.

To lessen the evils of intemperance, which can only be done by the substitution of the non-intoxicating mild beverages for those now in use, is worthy of the highest aim of the philanthropist. While prosecuting this noble purpose, the vineyardist may felicitate himself that in augmenting his earthly stores he is conferring benefits on mankind. Vine culture will do this, and a mild climate, genial soil, a healthful and plentiful country invite laborers.

Appendix A.

Exhibitors of Fruits Cultivated in the State of Virginia at the Biennial Meeting of the American Pomological Society at Richmond, Va., Sept. 7th, 1871.

Franklin Davis & Co., Richmond, Va. 193 varieties apples; 31 varieties pears; 2 varieties peaches.

H. R. Robey, Fredericksburg, Va. 6 varieties grapes; 23 apples; 22 pears.

Wm. O. Hurt, Bedford Co., Va. 51 varieties apples.

H. C. Williams, Fairfax Co., Va. 37 varieties apples; 11 pears; 12 cultivated grapes; 6 varieties native grapes.

Henry B. Jones, Brownsburg, Rockbridge Co., Va. 110 varieties of apples; 10 varieties pears; 10 peaches.

G. F. B. Leighton, Norfolk, Va. 8 varieties pears, including magnificent specimens of the Duchess d'Angouleme, some of which weighed 30½ ounces; also Seckels very large.

Tyree Dollins, Albemarle Co., Va. 135 varieties apples.

George W. Purvis, Nelson Co., Va. 5 varieties seedling peaches; 1 of apples; 1 plate of Catawba grapes.

C. Gillingham, Fairfax Co., Va. 18 varieties apples, and 21 varieties pears.

J. W. Porter, Albemarle Co., Va. 4 varieties of grapes; 11 of apples.

Potomac Fruit-Growers' Association, Washington, D. C. 18 varieties of apples; 54 of pears; 3 of grapes, and 1 of figs.

D. O. Munson, Fairfax Co., Va. A fine collection of apples and pears.

Appendix B.

Fruits exhibited by the Potomac Fruit-Growers' Association in Washington, D.C., September 3, 1872. First Annual Exhibition.

This was a magnificent display of fruits cultivated in the vicinity of Washington City. For brevity the names of the fruits are omitted. Suffice it to say that the list contained everything to satisfy the most fastidious taste, and salable as market fruits. The following is an extract from the official report :—

William Saunders, Superintendent of the Experimental Garden of the Agricultural Department. 50 varieties of pears ; 40 varieties of grapes—the merits of which have been fully established.

John Saul, Washington. 38 varieties pears ; 15 grapes, fully tested.

H. C. Williams, Fairfax Co., Va. 36 varieties apples ; 12 varieties pears ; 5 peaches ; 12 varieties cultivated grapes ; 6 indigenous varieties ; 1 quince ; 1 almond, approved for 30 years in the Washington market.

S. H. Snowden, Fairfax Co., Va. 27 varieties apples ; 7 varieties peaches.

Judge J. H. Gray, Fairfax Co., Va. 1 quince ; 3 varieties grapes ; 1 variety apple, and 3 varieties of peaches.

R. A. Phillips, North Arlington, Va. A luscious and abundant collection of Concord grapes.

H. Amidon, Washington, D. C. Devereux and Iona grapes.

Dr. R. P. Darby, Uniontown, D. C. Portugal quince, apples, pears, peaches, and grapes, very fine.

Captain H. D. Smith, Arlington, Va. Fine peaches and grapes.

John T. Bramhall, Fall's Church, Va. 6 varieties grapes.

Chalkley Gillingham, Accotink, Fairfax Co., Va. 26 varieties apples ; 7 varieties peaches ; 15 varieties pears—popular, approved varieties.

D. O. Munson, Fall's Church, Fairfax Co., Va. 11 varieties peaches ; 2 varieties apples.

J. B. Clagett, Silver Spring, Md. A splendid collection of grapes ; 14 varieties of pears.

Col. S. F. Chamberlain, Waterford, Loudoun Co., Va. 11 varieties apples ; 4 varieties peaches.

Appendix C.

Wine Grapes for North Carolina and Virginia.

Saunders, of Washington, D. C., named Lenoir and Devereux as desirable wine grapes for the mountain region of North Carolina and Virginia. All American wines have been made from the Fox family of grapes, which are not adapted to wine making. The *vitis estivalis* possess the true characteristics of wine making—the grapes named belong to this species—both with regard to sugar and bouquet. The reason why they have not been grown is because they do not ripen north. But they can be grown on the Virginia and North Carolina hills, and should be for wine. It has long been supposed that we have not the European *oidium* here; but we have it, though comparatively innocuous. Our mildew is unlike it, being caused by excess of moisture, while the European mildew (oidium) is caused by want of moisture.*

LOUDOUN COUNTY, VA.,

Was formed in 1757 from Fairfax, and named in honor of the Earl of Loudoun, commander of the military affairs in America during the latter part of the French and Indian war.

Among its records are ancient deeds and curious wills, and the minutes of the county courts held in the "reign of George the Second, by the grace of God King of Great Britain," etc., and the name and signature of James Monroe, late President of the United States, often appear appended to his official acts as a magistrate of the county.

Loudoun is one of the counties embraced in the class known as the Piedmont counties, lying between the Blue Ridge Mountains and the "tide-water counties" of Virginia.

It is bounded on the north by the Potomac River, east by Fairfax County, south by Prince William and Fauquier Counties, and west by Clarke County. Virginia, and Jefferson County, West Virginia.

Its western limit extends along the top of the Blue Ridge from Ashby's Gap to the Potomac opposite Harper's Ferry, and the Potomac washes its entire northern bounds for forty miles.

Its area is 525 square miles. Its population 20,724, of which 5691 are colored, and chiefly employed as laborers. Its mountains are the Blue Ridge and its spurs for twenty-three miles on the west. The Catoctin Mountain, a low range parallel to and sixteen miles east of "the Ridge," and a low range called "the Short Hill" also parallel to and two miles east of "the Ridge" rising suddenly near Hillsboro' and running north nine miles to the Potomac, on the other side of which river it crosses Maryland and goes into Pennsylvania, where it rises into the "Kittany Mountains."

Between the Blue Ridge and the Catoctin is the far famed "Loudoun Valley."

The surface of the entire county is rolling, well drained, and without any swamps or miasmatic marshes, but stands drought well, as has been proved by the last three years.

The water courses are the Potomac and its tributaries. Goose Creek, Beaver Dam, the Catoctin and its forks, Little River, Tusca-

* Proceedings of the Thirteenth Session of the American Pomological Society, held in Richmond, Va., Sept. 6, 7, and 8, 1871, page 68.

rora, Sycolin, Broad Run, Sugar Land, Horse Pen, etc., all bold streams, pervading the whole county.

Besides these main streams there are few if any farms in every field of which there is not a spring or running water of pure and wholesome quality.

The soil of course varies, but blue grass is indigenous to the whole county, while timothy, clover, and other grasses are raised in luxuriance. All the cereals are produced in abundance, but corn is the largest and best paying crop.

Being eminently a grass country, *grazing* was, before the war, one of the largest and most profitable interests, and is now being revived more and more yearly, with the advantage of being little over a day's *drive*, or a few hours' run by rail, to the Alexandria, Georgetown, or Washington Markets, with easy, certain, and quick access to Baltimore, Philadelphia, or New York.

The *Dairy* is becoming an important interest, from the adaptation of the rich pasturage and springs to it, and the facility of shipping the milk and butter to market, while the "Old Dominion" cheese factory, at Hamilton, is turning out, yearly, a large stock of its manufacture, which is becoming one of the favorite cheeses in the markets.

Fruits of all kinds have long been cultivated for domestic use, and the product of the plum, cherry, peach, and apple trees of Loudoun have elicited and deserved the praise of all who have visited the county. All kinds of fruit are produced in great perfection; increasing attention is being paid to this culture. The grape grows here as naturally as in the Rhine valley. The slopes of the Blue Ridge, of the Catoctin, and of "the Hills" are specially adapted for vineyards. The grape, as fruit, or in wine or brandy, is an interest of increasing value.

Sheep thrive well and pay well here, and there are a number of the best stocks; the Blue Ridge mutton cannot be surpassed in England.

The *Temperature* being even, rarely hotter than 85° or colder than 8° Fahrenheit, and very seldom reaching either of these extremes, the summers are not oppressive, and the winters are open. Cattle graze until Christmas, and much plowing is done in January.

About one-third of the county is in timber. Limestone underlies the greater part of it, and lime for fertilizing is easily accessible to every farmer, and acts most happily on the soil in conjunction with clover and plaster.

Iron, copper, and barytes have been found and mined. The Potomac Furnace, opposite the Point of Rocks, was started half a century ago, and has been supplied with ore from the adjacent lands. The iron interest offers a large field for profitable investment.

On the western slope of the Catoctin Mountain is a deposit of white marble, extending north and south for over ten miles, with a breadth in some places of 2000 feet, cropping out at many points, and hundreds of feet in depth. The Virginia Marble Company is engaged in opening and developing a quarry; the lessee has expended $50,000 in the enterprise. The marble is white and fine, equal to the Vermont marble, while in places there is a solid vein of flesh colored. This is a very important interest.

There are various mineral springs in Loudoun; one near Purcellville, known as Silcott's Spring, is a place of large resort with benefit to invalids; a fine chalybeate spring near Middleburg; a strong sulphur spring near Farmwell Station; a chalybeate at Leesburg; one near Hamilton, and at other points.

The people of the county are plain, steady, intelligent, independent, and kind; of German, Irish, Quaker, Scottish, and English stocks.

There is little poverty, and but few instances of great wealth, yet if a stranger were to judge of the condition of the people from the number of handsome and fashionably dressed ladies, and the fine display of horses and carriages to be seen at the annual county " Fair and Cattle Show" held at Leesburg, he would say "Loudoun is *certainly* prosperous."

Notwithstanding the numerous other means of transportation possessed by this county, there were shipped to Loudoun over the Washington and Ohio Rail Road alone, in 1871, 35 handsome carriages and 14 pianos; and in 1872, 27 carriages and 10 pianos.

Nearly all, male and female, give their personal attention to, or take part in, the work of the farm or house, and the exhibition of the results of domestic industry at the annual fair is one of the most attractive features.

White laborers readily meet with employment, and are treated with respect if deserving.

Nearly every farm is owned by its occupant.

The chief architectural ornaments of the county are " Oak Hill," built by James Monroe, late President of the United States, now owned by Doctor Quinby, late of the city of New York; "Oatlands," the residence of George Carter; " Belmont," built by the late Ludwell Lee (where Gen. LaFayette made his home during his visit to Loudoun in 1825), now owned by Hon. F. P. Stanton, of Washington; and a dwelling just completed, near Leesburg, by C. R. Paxton, Esq., of

Bloomsburg, Pennsylvania, at a cost of $100,000, probably the most complete, convenient, and substantial dwelling in the State.

Generally, the houses in the county are unostentatious buildings of frame, brick, or stone, planned for use and durability rather than show, but, with their plentiful gardens, spring houses, cool shades, and rich fields, they present as perfect a picture of home comfort and independence as can be found in any land.

There are numerous churches of various denominations. There are 55 free schools, in which are taught 3210 scholars, of which 652 are colored. These have 60 teachers (8 colored), and are supported by the State and county. Besides these there are numerous private academies and schools in the county.

The streams supply about 80 flouring and grist mills, and the water power on the river and its tributaries is ample for every kind of manufacture. The "Big Spring," near Leesburg, supplied a flouring mill on the Potomac (burned during the war), which turned out daily 80 to 100 barrels and employed but little of the power. There are 2 woollen factories, but all kinds of factories are needed, and none would be more successful than a straw paper mill, and a wholesale shoe factory, as there are many tanneries in the county which send their products to Baltimore.

The average annual value of the marketable products of Loudoun are about $1,500,000 to $1,750,000 which could be increased 50 per cent. or more by concentrating care and culture on smaller tracts, and by studying the peculiar needs of the lands, making each field a speciality.

The accessibility to market is a great advantage to this county.

In price the lands vary according to location and improvements, from $5 to $100 per acre; the average is about $25. There are many " new comers" from the Northern States, from England and Scotland, and all are eagerly welcomed.

The county roads are good, and, annually, an average sum of $12,000 is expended on them. There are turnpikes crossing the county from east to west from Washington, Georgetown, and Alexandria, to Winchester *via* Aldie; Middleburg, Ashby's Gap, and *via* Leesburg and Snickersville; a turnpike, north and south, from Aldie to Leesburg; another from Waterford to Point of Rocks on the Potomac; another from Purcellville, on the Winchester and Leesburg Pike, to the Potomac opposite Berlin, and another from Hillsboro to Harper's Ferry.

The Chesapeake and Ohio Canal extends on the Maryland side the whole length of the north side of Loudoun, with one lift lock opposite

Leesburg, and another opposite the southeast corner of the county, giving access to boats loaded on the Virginia shore, and thus furnishing the county with Cumberland coal, lumber, etc., and shipping wheat and other grains to the Georgetown and Alexandria markets. The Baltimore and Ohio Rail Road skirts the county for 12 miles from Harper's Ferry to the Point of Rocks, which place is 12 miles from Leesburg and 69 miles from Baltimore. The Metropolitan Rail Road runs from Point of Rocks to Washington City on the Maryland side.

The Washington and Ohio Rail Road crosses the county from near Guilford on the east to Snickersville on the west. It is completed and running to Hamilton, seven miles west of Leesburg, and forty-four miles from Alexandria. In a short time the road will be running to Purcellville, three miles further west. So soon as the Washington and Ohio Rail Road is completed to the Valley at Winchester, to the coal-fields of Hampshire and Hardy Counties, the timber lands of West Virginia, and to the Ohio River, it will place Loudoun on the great artery of the Union east and west.

Its resources on the surface and under the surface, *as yet hardly conceived of or touched*, will be developed. Its inexhaustible wealth, and its facilities for transportation, will attract intelligent immigration and capital, which its people are longing to welcome.

The easy, short, and frequent railroad connections make this county a suburb of Alexandria, Washington, and Baltimore, and put it within a few hours of Philadelphia and New York.

Numbers of the citizens of the District of Columbia are seeking permanent homes here, while many more find health and renewed life in its cool and quiet retreats in summer. Among the most prominent enterprises are the erection of summer resorts on the Blue Ridge and in the beautiful region of its base.

Taking into consideration the climate, temperature, health, scenery, water, soil, population, and resources of Loudoun, with its close and certain connection with all the markets and cities of the seaboard, there is no region where the average of human comfort is higher than in it. Other regions may excel it in some one particular, but none combine more of all the elements of peace, plenty, happiness, and independence, than Loudoun.

The Washington and Ohio Rail Road has five stations in Loudoun County, viz., Guilford, Farmwell, Leesburg, Clark's Gap, and Hamilton; to these will shortly be added three others—Round Hill, Purcellville, and Snickersville.

GUILFORD STATION is twenty-seven miles from Alexandria, in the centre of a thrifty and stirring community. The States of Pennsylvania, New York, New Jersey, and California are represented at and in its immediate vicinity by substantial citizens, who, having purchased farms, have united with their Virginia neighbors in developing the resources of this portion of Loudoun County. Old England and South America have also contributed to the population by the immigration of farmers of means and ability. The villages of Gum Spring, Arcola, and Daysville receive their supplies and ship their productions at Guilford Station.

FARMWELL STATION is thirty-one miles from Alexandria. The neighborhood of which Farmwell is the depot has experienced the good results arising from a healthy immigration, and, like Guilford, is greatly improved in its increased productions and in the character and intelligence of the people. This depot receives the supplies and ships the products of the villages of Belmont, Frankville, and Brookland. On the lands of the late Doctor Lee, near this station, there is a strong sulphur spring.

LEESBURG is the county seat of Loudoun and a station on the Washington and Ohio Rail Road. It lies at the eastern base of the Catoctin Mountains, one and a half miles from the Potomac River, at Ball's Bluff, and thirty-seven and a half miles from Alexandria, Georgetown, and Washington. It was established in 1758, and has a population of 1800. Its streets are at right angles, well paved and lighted. An ample and permanent supply of pure water is carried by pipes throughout the town. Two newspapers are published here.' Its buildings are of stone, brick, and frame, substantial and comfortable. The assessed value of the real estate in the town is $444,290; it has a telegraph line to Alexandria, along the line of the Washington and Ohio Rail Road. There are six churches, of various denominations, including two colored; the other public buildings are the Depot of the Washington and Ohio Rail Road, the Bank, Academy, Court House, Jail, Circuit and County Court Clerk's Offices, two free schools, one for white and one for colored children, two female academies, two hotels, and numerous stores, restaurants, and boarding-houses; the stores keep a complete stock of all articles, as various, tasteful, and cheap as can be had in a city. There is a large foundry and steam saw-mill, planing-mill, and agricultural machine factory.

The Loudoun Agricultural Society hold a fair and cattle show annually at Leesburg, which is numerously attended and well supported.

Leesburg is one of the most healthful places in the Union. Its people are well educated, hospitable, and social.

A daily line of stages connect with the Washington and Ohio Rail Road, at Leesburg, for Aldie and Middleburg.

CLARK'S GAP, four miles west of Leesburg, is a very important station. It drains a splendid country for many miles; is three and a half miles south of Waterford, a very thriving Quaker settlement, having a population of 419. There is a fine road from Waterford to the depot at the Gap. Waterford is in Jefferson Township, which contains 3355 inhabitants, and has two fine merchant mills, which do a large business.

HAMILTON STATION, forty-four miles from Alexandria and six and a half miles west of Leesburg, is the present western terminus of the Washington and Ohio Rail Road, an important station, with a constantly growing trade; is situated in a rich and populous country, an intelligent and wealthy community, with fine and productive farms. This station is the business centre for the neighboring villages of Hillsboro, Purcellville, Wheatland, Union, Mountsville, Philomont, Pot House (New Lisbon), Snickersville, Lincoln, Hughesville, Bloomfield, and Circleville, to which is added the large business of eight fine merchant mills.

The Old Dominion Cheese Factory at Hamilton, a new enterprise, is in successful operation, and in 1872, the second year of its existence, manufactured 2100 boxes. The home demand alone is greater than could be supplied by half a dozen establishments of similar extent.

The *Loudoun Enterprise,* a well-conducted newspaper, is published at Hamilton.

Frequent public sales of cattle are held at Hamilton; and the well-known character of the stock raised in Loudoun attracts the lovers of fine stock, not only from the adjoining counties, but from the cities of Washington and Baltimore.

In the vicinity of Hamilton Depot there is a mineral spring; the water possesses cathartic and alterative virtues, and is doubtless as good as many other well known mineral waters.

Western-bound passengers take Kemp's line of stages at Hamilton for Purcellville and Snickersville in Loudoun, Berryville in Clarke, and Winchester in Frederick counties.

FRUIT CULTURE AND DAIRY FARMING.

Attention is invited to the following paper, contributed by Col. S. E. Chamberlin, of the Department of Agriculture, Washington, D. C.

Col. Chamberlin, late of the United States Army, came to Virginia a few years ago from the State of New York, and is extensively engaged in these branches of trade at Waterford, in the county of Loudoun.

The region known as the "Piedmont Region," extending from the head of tide to the "Blue Ridge," deriving its name from the "foot of the mountain," has peculiar and special adaptation to the successful cultivation of the fruit-tree.

Loudoun County forms a conspicuous part of this region, the soil possessing the happy combination formed from greenstone, quartz, gneiss, and clay-slate, constituting that rich, durable soil, for healthy growth and long life to the tree, so desirable; the climate being especially favorable, with spring not so early as to force premature budding, to be injured by following frosts, and with fall sufficiently late to permit the apple, pear, and peach to ripen in perfection, with size, form, and flavor unequalled in any part of the world. The attention of some of our most eminent pomologists and extensive fruit-growers has been directed to the superior advantages offered here for growing fruit, for not only home, but for foreign markets. The age that the apple, peach, and pear trees attain is wonderful. They do not come into bearing as early as in lighter soils, but are far more productive; and many of the diseases so fatal to, in particular, the peach and pear in more northern districts, are avoided. The "Yellows," that has proved so destructive to the peach orchards of New Jersey, Delaware, Maryland, Pennsylvania, and in our more southern States, is unknown. Peach trees thirty, forty, and fifty years, and many *known* to be even older, are found healthy and vigorous, bearing fruit every year. At the last session of the American Pomological Society, held at Richmond, September, 1871, the various fruits of this locality were freely discussed and compared with those from all parts of the United States, and pronounced inferior to none. The eminent pomologist, Charles Downing, said "that the 'Piedmont Region' of Virginia was the best fruit-growing country in the world." Many valuable varieties of our apples, among them the Abram, Baltzby, Bentley Sweet, Bowling's Sweet, Holladay, Limbertwig, Magnum, Ogleby, Peck's Pleasant, Rawle's Janet (or Rock Ramon), Red Winter Sweet, Roberson's White, Robey's Seedling, and Fall

5

Queen, have their origin in this region. Many other valuable seed-lings, among them the Loudoun Pippin, Round Hill Pippin, and Whitescarver, from this locality, are becoming familiar to pomolo-gists, and find high favor wherever known.

But little attention has been given to the cultivation of fruit for market, and less to the selection of such varieties as are suitable to the climate; although favored by a most genial climate, and a soil rich in all the elements of food for the tree, it is necessary to select such kinds as are acclimated; and here our great advantage lies, for by careful and proper selection many of the varieties most desirable for market can be grown to perfection defying competition elsewhere. Downing says: "unfavorable soil and climate are powerful agents in deteriorating varieties of fruit trees." Many of the orchards where trees were selected without regard to their adaptation to our climate, but bought of northern nurserymen as the most valuable varieties of the north, have proven almost worthless. Apples that mature at the north in the warm summer months are improved when brought here; those maturing late when removed south prove a failure, thus proving that it is impossible to pass certain natural limits of fitness for cli-mate. Along our highways the apple, peach, pear, and cherry are found; though neglected and permitted to grow undisturbed, they are found growing vigorously and bearing profusely, many showing great age, giving conclusive evidence of the particular adaptation of our soil and climate to their growth. The decaying calcareous rock, with a warm dry soil naturally well drained, the grape and all small fruits find a congenial home. The Catawba grape, so long and favor-ably known throughout our whole country, was *first discovered* in this region. The blackberry and raspberry are here found, which for size and flavor are unequalled by the best cultivated specimens.

Loudoun County, lying at the door of our Nation's Capital, with ready communication with the East, West, North, and South, offers greater inducements to the fruit-grower for the successful and profit-able growing of fruit, than can be found in any other locality in the United States.

DAIRY farming in Loudoun County is destined to become one of our leading industries. The natural advantages are such as to offer every inducement for such enterprise. The dairy has become an im-portant branch of national industry. It is rapidly spreading over new fields. It is engaging the attention of farmers in the Western, Northwestern, and Middle States; and wherever lands are adapted to grazing, where there are streams of living water, dairy farming is taking the lead of all other branches. In the State of New York alone the dairy products are valued at more than one hundred million dollars annually, far exceeding in value the grain crop. The consumption of cheese in this country is increasing. We are *exporting* but little more than in 1861, while the production has increased from 103,000,000 to 240,000.000 of pounds in 1869. The average increase of home consumption has been at the rate of 13,000,000 of pounds per year.

Nature has furnished Loudoun with all the requisite elements for success in this calling. With our pure air, our green hills, our never-failing springs of sparkling ice-cold water, to be found on every farm, with abundance of shade from the oak, hickory, walnut, and maple, with the sweetest of all grasses, we may challenge the world to excel us in the manufacture of rich sweet butter and cheese. Among the rich succulent grasses indigenous to our soil the blue grass (Poa pratensis) takes the lead. An eminent agricultural writer says of this grass: " Whoever has blue grass has the basis of all agricultural prosperity; and that man, if he have not the finest horses, cattle, and sheep, has no one to blame but himself. Others, in other circumstances, may do as well. He can hardly avoid doing well if he will try! White clover (Trifolium repens) and Red-top or Herdsgrass (Agrostis vulgaris) are among our native grasses, and Timothy (Phleum pratense), the most valuable of all grasses, was introduced into England *from Virginia* by Peter Wynche about the years 1760 or 1761.

Our people have almost everything to learn in the proper manner of making butter and preparing it for market. So soon as this can be acquired, and our farms stocked with good cows, everything will prosper. One of the best markets in our country, Washington, the thirteenth city in size in the United States by the last census, and rapidly growing, with an increasing demand for the very best dairy products, at fancy prices, will consume all we can furnish.

The manufacture of CHEESE has commenced in our county, and an article has been produced commanding an excellent price, pronounced by competent judges unequalled in flavor by that made anywhere else. As to the successful manufacture of cheese in Loudoun County, I submit the following extract from the United States Agricultural Report for 1871:—

" DAIRYING IN VIRGINIA.

" Several cheese factories have recently been erected in Virginia, and an increased number may be expected at an early day. No State promises a better profit for capital invested in associated dairying. The Old Dominion cheese factory at Hamilton, Loudoun County, Virginia, was established in May, 1871. The amount of milk received from May 6 to September 8 was 378,138 pounds; amount of cheese manufactured, 36,625 pounds; average quantity of milk required for one pound of cheese, 10.3 pounds; average value of cheese at the factory, 12¼ cents per pound, the product being of excellent quality, notwithstanding the severe drought of the season. The superintendent, Mr. J. K. Taylor, says that it must be conceded that Virginia is admirably adapted to dairying, and that the production of milk, butter, and cheese would pay the farmers of the State vastly better than the present exhaustive system of cropping with grain and tobacco.

" Mr. Taylor, reporting on the sales of cheese, butter, milk, and calves from his dairy of eight cows, for the season commencing May 7, and closing December 12, states the net receipts over current expenses at $387.19, averaging $48.40 per cow. From Mr. T. R. Smith's dairy of ten cows, near Lincoln, Loudoun County, 2640 pounds of cheese were made during the season of 1871, netting $273.81. Amount of butter made, 970 pounds, bringing an average price of 30 cents per pound; value of ten calves, $61.40 ; average return per cow, without deduction for cost of manufacturing butter, $62.62. Mr. E. J. Smith's dairy, near Lincoln, varying from ten to eleven cows, reports an average of $46.03 per cow for the season, without deduction for cost of making butter. Mr. B. W. Welsh's dairy, near Circleville, in the same county, reports an average return of $43 per cow.

" The low price of land in Virginia, in comparison with the best dairy districts in Pennsylvania and New York, the abundance and quality of grasses in the best locations, the length of the grazing season, and the comparatively small amount of winter forage required, combine to render the business profitable here. Improvement in the milking qualities of cows, and a better acquaintance with their proper management, will increase the cash value of the product per cow, which is now comparatively low."

CLARKE COUNTY, VA.

This county was formed in 1836 from Frederick; is seventeen miles long and fifteen wide ; lies in the northeast part of the great valley of Virginia, between Loudoun and Frederick—the former county forming its eastern and the latter its western boundary.

The Shenandoah River passes through the southern and eastern portions of the county at the foot of the Blue Ridge, and the Opequon near its western line. The county is intersected by a number of small streams which furnish water-power for manufacturing purposes.

For its area, Clarke probably contains more fine land than any county in the State. The surface is beautifully diversified; the soil is based on blue limestone, with a fine growth of timber, and is very productive. The farms, generally large, have good buildings, and are in a good state of cultivation. It produces large crops of wheat, corn, etc., and is a fine cattle region. The census of 1870 shows the population to be 7655.

When reached by the Washington and Ohio Rail Road, the agricultural productions of this rich county, and its deposit of valuable iron ores, will materially contribute to the business of the road and the prosperity of the county. The Shenandoah River is lined with ores of a superior quality, which must reach tide-water at Alexandria, either in ore or pig metal, by means of the Washington and Ohio Rail Road.

These deposits are on the line of the railroad, nineteen miles west of Hamilton Station and sixty-two miles from Alexandria, at which point the iron can be shipped to any point required. The Shannondale Furnace, in Jefferson County, is on these deposits, as is also the Shenandoah Iron Works, in Page County, which recently sold for $240,000.

There are good turnpikes and county roads in all directions. The Baltimore and Ohio Rail Road passes through the northeast corner of the county. It has a depot at Wade's, seven miles from Berryville, and one at Summit Point, in the adjoining county of Jefferson, about the same distance from Berryville.

BERRYVILLE, the county seat, is a handsome village, centrally located, and commands a fine view of the Blue Ridge Mountains; is twelve miles east from Winchester, and sixty miles west from Alexandria; contains the usual county buildings, five churches, schools. machine shop, and agricultural works, coach factory, wagon makers, flour and grist mills (water powers). Population, 580. Is in Battletown township, which contains 2464 inhabitants.

The stage line between Hamilton Station and Winchester passes through Clarke County, *via* Berryville, daily.

GREENWAY COURT, the seat of the late Lord Fairfax, is in this county, thirteen miles southeast from Winchester, near the village of White Post. Greenway Court was recently partially destroyed by fire.

Leaving the western limit of Loudoun, the line of the Washington and Ohio Rail Road enters Clarke County at the summit of the

" Blue Ridge," and, crossing the Shenandoah River at Grigsby's Island, runs through the county in nearly a westerly line for fifteen miles.

JEFFERSON COUNTY, W. VA.,

Was formed in 1801 from Berkley County. Its mean length is 22 miles, breadth 12 miles. The Potomac River forms its northeastern border. The Shenandoah enters the county near its southeastern boundary, and flowing in a northeastern direction, parallel with the " Blue Ridge," enters the Potomac at Harper's Ferry.

The face of the country is rolling, and the soil equal in fertility to that of any county in the State. This county is thickly settled, highly improved, and wealthy.

Shepherdstown, the county seat, is situated on the Potomac River, in the northwestern part of the county, 12 miles above Harper's Ferry, and contains 1389 inhabitants.

Charlestown, the former county seat, is on the line of railroad from Winchester to Harper's Ferry, 8 miles from the latter, and 22 from the former. Is a pleasant and flourishing town, containing 1593 inhabitants.

Harper's Ferry is 30 miles from Winchester, 57 miles from Washington and Alexandria, and 81 from Baltimore. It is connected by rail with Baltimore and Winchester. Has great manufacturing advantages. Until the year 1861 the United States government had an armory and arsenal in operation here, but being destroyed in the early part of the war (1861), they have not been replaced.

The Shannondale Springs, on the Shenandoah River, near the " Blue Ridge" are easy of access, via Charlestown, from which place they are 5 miles distant.

The Washington and Ohio Rail Road runs a few miles south of the southern line of Jefferson County, and must draw largely of its resources. According to the census of 1870 the population of this county is 16,562. It has eleven post-offices.

FREDERICK COUNTY, VA.,

Lies west of Clarke, and its western line forms the eastern boundary of Hampshire County, West Virginia. It was created in 1738, is about 25 miles long, with a mean width of 18 miles; area 378 square miles.

The Opequon, Sleepy, and Back Creeks rise in this county and flow into the Potomac. The principal elevation is the North Mountain, extending along the west border. Is one of the most wealthy and highly cultivated counties in the valley of Virginia. Every farmer in this county has its springs or stream. Water power is very abundant, and there are now in operation about sixty flouring mills, several woollen mills, and other manufacturing establishments. Blue limestone underlies a large portion of the surface. There are 75,000 acres of limestone land, capable of producing one million bushels of wheat; eight turnpike roads connect these with the town of Winchester, making it *the* centre for this whole area, and likewise a depot, to a great extent, for the products of the renowned Shenandoah Valley.

Winchester is the county seat. It contains 4477 inhabitants; is 75 miles from Alexandria and Washington, and 113 from Baltimore; is well and substantially built; the streets cross each other at right angles, and are generally paved; the houses are mostly built of brick or stone. It has churches of various denominations and schools, and is a delightful place of residence. Winchester is on the railroad leading from Baltimore *via* Harper's Ferry, to Strasburg, Shenandoah County, 19 miles distant, where it connects with the Manassas Branch of the Orange, Alexandria, and Manassas Rail Road, running from Alexandria to Harrisonburg in Rockingham County. There is a fine McAdamized turnpike road from Winchester to Staunton, *via* Strasburg, New Market, and Harrisonburg, a distance of 95 miles in the southwest.

From Clarke County the route of the Washington and Ohio Rail Road is through Frederick, *via* Winchester, for about 25 miles. After leaving Winchester, the line passes through Petticoat Gap in the Little North Mountain, and reaches the summit of the Great North Mountain at Lockhardt's Gap with easy grades, thence by Capper's Spring (now called Rock Enon) and Capon Spring to Hampshire County, West Virginia.

The importance of the Washington and Ohio Rail Road to the town of Winchester may be inferred from the fact that in addition to a subscription of thirty thousand dollars to its capital stock, the same to become available on the road reaching its corporate limits, its town council have granted it free right of way through the town, and have agreed to purchase, without cost to the company, land within its limits sufficient for the erection of repair and workshops.

The Washington and Ohio Rail Road will here connect with railways, now in rapid construction, which extend through that valley into the States of North Carolina, Kentucky, Tennessee, and the whole southwest. It is besides only 97 miles east of the great coal fields which will be cut through by the main line of the road all the way from the Alleghanies to the Ohio River.

Newtown (Stephensburg) is a neat and thriving village, 8 miles south of Winchester, on the McAdamized road to Staunton, and contains 625 inhabitants. Stephensburg was established by law in 1758, and was settled almost exclusively by Germans whose descendants long preserved the customs and language of their ancestors.

Middletown is 5 miles south of Stephensburg, on the Staunton Road, the finest in the State.

Jordan's White Sulphur Springs are located in the northeastern portion of the beautiful valley of the Shenandoah 5 miles from Winchester; and one and a half miles from Stephenson's Depot on the Harper's Ferry and Winchester Branch of the Baltimore and Ohio Rail Road.

Jordan's is a place of great resort, and has accommodations for several hundred visitors. The waters resemble the celebrated Greenbrier White Sulphur Springs of Virginia.

The county of Frederick has seventeen post offices, and, according to the census of 1870, contains a population of 17,221.

HAMPSHIRE COUNTY, W. VA.,

Lies west of Frederick County, Virginia, was established in 1754, and prior to the formation of Mineral County, it contained an area of 850 square miles. Hampshire is drained by the north and south branches of the Potomac, the Potomac River, and the great Cacapon. Its surface is occupied by the valleys and ridges of the Alleghany chain of mountains. The valleys are wide, fertile, and well improved. Hampshire is a fine grazing, grain farming, and wool growing county, and contains extensive beds of coal and iron ore. The streams afford unsurpassed water-power. This county contains over 500,000 acres of arable land, of which about one-fifth are under cultivation. These figures include Mineral County, recently formed out of it. Prior to this the assessed value of farms was $4,000,000, and it is not doubted that a much larger sum could now be obtained for them. On the authority of Mr. Dodge, of the United States Agricultural Department, it is claimed that this county takes the lead in horses, cows, corn, buckwheat, and the products of the dairy; and there is no doubt that its prosperity has been materially assisted and enhanced by its proximity to the Baltimore and Ohio Rail Road.

On the road leading from Winchester, a few miles east of Romney, there is a deposit of glass sand found in a gap in the mountain. An immense amount of sand rock is exposed in the narrow pass, which, in places, is very soft and worn by the elements into narrow caves. In parts of these soft places the sand is remarkably white and pure, and is unquestionably a superior article for glass making.

A citizen of Reading, Pennsylvania, has recently purchased, on northern account, a body of land in this county, near Rock Enon Spring, six miles in length, containing a deposit of the best quality of iron ore. A vein of 16 feet has already been opened, and it is expected that several furnaces will shortly be in operation. Until the Washington and Ohio Rail Road reaches these deposits the iron will have to be transported, in wagons, to Winchester, a distance of about 15 miles, and it will pay even at that.

ROMNEY, the county seat, is a thriving town on the south branch of the Potomac, in the heart of the county, 40 miles west of Winchester. Is reached from Green Spring Depot, 163 miles from Baltimore, and New Creek Station, 201 miles from Baltimore, by the Baltimore and Ohio Rail Road. Population 482. The Parkersburg Turnpike passes through Romney.

CAPPER'S SPRING, now called Rock Enon, on the west side of North Mountain, two miles from Capon, and five miles nearer Alexandria and Washington than Capon, is second to none in the State for its medicinal qualities. Though yet comparatively little known, these springs are destined to rival, successfully, the most popular of the many watering places of Virginia.

These springs have been recently purchased by a number of gentlemen, residing in the District of Columbia, by whom they have been refitted and put in fine order for visitors. The extension of the Washington and Ohio Rail Road will render them exceedingly valuable, the waters being highly prized.

"CAPON SPRINGS" are in the productive valley of the Cacapon River, on the west side of the North Mountain, 30 miles from Winchester, and one mile from the Washington and Ohio Rail Road, a place of great resort during the summer months. The buildings are commodious, accommodating one thousand visitors, and the grounds extensive.

ICE MOUNTAIN, 26 miles northwest from Winchester, is a curiosity worthy of mention. At the western base of the mountain, which is here

about 700 feet high and very precipitous, is an area of 100 yards in
length and a breadth of 30 feet up the mountain side, covered with
loose rocks, under which at all seasons of the year blocks of ice of
several pounds weight may be found. Butter or fresh meats are preserved here almost indefinitely. At the base of this bed of ice flows
a spring of intensely cold water, and yet these rocks are exposed to
the rays of the sun after nine o'clock in the morning.

The HANGING ROCKS, near Romney, are notable curiosities. Here
the river has cut its way through a mountain of about 500 feet in
height. The boldness of the rocks and the wildness of the scene excite
"awe in the beholder."

CAUDY'S CASTLE, a most stupendous work of nature, was so named
from having been the retreat of an early settler when pursued by the
Indians.

The TEA TABLE is about 10 miles from Caudy's Castle. This table
is of solid rock, and presents the form of "a man's hat standing on
its crown." It is about four feet in height and the same in diameter.
From the top issues a clear stream of water which flows over the brim
on all sides and forms a fountain of exquisite beauty.

Coal and iron abound in this county.

The population of Hampshire County is 8125. It has sixteen post-
offices.

The Washington and Ohio Rail Road passes into the State of West
Virginia at the southern edge of Hampshire County, and that a
greater increase in its productive wealth and resources will result
from its establishment on its lower boundary must be apparent to any
one conversant with the vivifying power of railroads.

E. Sheets, Esq., of Reading, Pennsylvania, writes to the President
of the Washington and Ohio Rail Road from Boston, under date of
January 8, 1873, as follows: "Your letter of the 3d inst. is before me,
forwarded from Reading. I do think that the Washington and Ohio
Rail Road will be one of the best paying roads in this country. I
would offer to transport at least 150,000 tons of ore and material,
yearly, from the lands I hold myself, and from those of the friends for
whom I am acting." The lands containing this deposit of iron ore lie
near Rock Enon Springs in this county, on the line of the Washington
and Ohio Rail Road.

HARDY COUNTY, W. VA.,

Was formed in 1786 from Hampshire, and named in honor of
Samuel Hardy, a member of Congress from 1783 to 1785. Until
its limits were reduced by the formation of Grant County, its length
was 42 miles, and its breadth 17 miles. It adjoins Hampshire on the
south, and is intersected by the South Branch of the Potomac, which,
in its passage through the county, receives two affluents called the
North and South Forks; it is also drained by the Cacapon and Lost
Rivers. The surface is very mountainous, and abounds in mineral
wealth: the soil of the valleys is very fertile. It is in many respects
one of the most remarkable counties in the State of West Virginia.
It is sufficient to say that its fecundity is becoming proverbial, and
that better land can nowhere be found in the United States. Is particularly famous for its productiveness as a corn region. On the river
bottoms lands have been planted for consecutive years with this grain
ever since the advent of the first white settlers, and the Indians are
reported to have raised the same crop upon them for ages previously.
Notwithstanding this continuous drain upon the resources of the soil,
by cropping with one staple, it shows no sign of failing, but produces
as luxuriantly now as it did one hundred years ago. With a highly
productive soil, attractive scenery, splendid cattle and horses, a kind
and hospitable people, it cannot but entice thousands of settlers to
its borders.

Cattle-feeding is the chief pursuit of the farmers. The great distance from market renders this the most profitable pursuit, but the
Washington and Ohio Rail Road will supply the much needed transportation, and will cause this valley to be one of the garden spots of
our country.

At the Capon iron furnace, about four miles south of Wardensville,
an article of the first quality is manufactured, which is sold in Philadelphia for boiler making. This article now incurs the expense of 16
miles wagon transportation to the railroad at Strasburg, but on the
Washington and Ohio Rail Road reaching the furnace this important
item will be saved to the manufacturer. The ore used by this furnace
is a continuation of the Pennsylvania Juniata iron ore beds: they
have been long worked and are known to be good.

MOOREFIELD, the county seat, is a town of considerable ambition.
It contains probably 1500 inhabitants, and has one of the finest
hotels in the Valley of Virginia. Is pleasantly situated on low
ground near the junction of the South Fork with the South Branch

of the Potomac, contains a number of good modern style buildings, and a number in course of erection. The situation of Moorefield, with respect to the surrounding country, will inevitably make it a place of considerable commercial importance.

The mountain lands are generally in a state of nature, covered with the original growth of timber. This whole region is favored with water power. All the streams above Moorefield have a remarkably uniform rapid descent, so that nearly every half mile would furnish an excellent water power for ordinary purposes. These streams are supplied by permanent springs, and even when the season is quite dry there is an ample supply of water.

Moorefield is 27 miles from Romney, in Hampshire County, 42 miles from Franklin, in Pendleton County, and 132 miles from Washington, D. C.

Leaving Capon Springs, in Hampshire County, and passing through the valley to a point one and a half miles beyond the town of Wardensville, in this county, the line of the Washington and Ohio Rail Road will pass through Sandy Ridge by one of the grandest and most picturesque gaps in the mountains of Virginia. Following the valley of Lost River and its tributary streams, the South Branch Mountain is reached, and descending the western slope we arrive at the town of Moorefield, the county seat of Hardy, in the great South Branch valley. From Moorefield the Baltimore and Ohio Rail Road is distant on the north nearly 50 miles, and the Chesapeake and Ohio Rail Road, the nearest on the south, more than 100 miles distant.

This road will place the South Branch Valley 71 miles nearer market, besides saving more than one-half the present wagon transportation. By a branch 30 miles long from Moorefield to Piedmont, it shortens the distance to tide water for the Cumberland coal 31 miles.

Concerning Lost River, Mr. Dodge, before quoted, says:—

"LOST RIVER is one of the wonders of nature. After coursing through a fertile valley for twenty-five miles, it breaks through the Lost River Mountains and bursts the barriers of Timber Ridge, and then encounters a new obstacle in Sandy Ridge, which it passes by a curious piece of fluvial strategy, mining its way among the loose rocks of the underlying strata, but loses itself in its subterranean meanderings of three miles, coming to the light again rather in the capacity of strong springs than as the powerful current of a river that has lost its way, to become anew the source of a considerable stream—the Cacapon."

A subscription of one hundred and fifty thousand dollars to the capital stock of the Washington and Ohio Rail Road Company is expected from this county, to become available on the road reaching its border.

Hardy County has eight post-offices, and a population of 5518.

GRANT COUNTY, W. VA.,

Was formed in 1868 from Hardy, and named in honor of Gen. Ulysses S. Grant, now President of the United States. It lies in the north-eastern portion of the State, and joins Hardy on the west, which county it resembles in its general features; is a small county, and divided into three townships, called Grant, Milroy, and Union; is watered by the north and south branches of the Potomac and their tributaries. The surface of the county is mountainous, with smooth valleys and table lands; is a fine corn-growing and cattle region, producing splendid cattle and horses; is intersected by the north-western and other turnpikes.

A heavy deposit of coal exists on Red Creek and also on Stoney River, a branch of the north branch of the Potomac, in this county. An extensive purchase of coal lands was recently made in this vicinity. Population in 1870, 4467.

Grant Court House, the county seat, is centrally located, 30 miles from New Creek Station, Baltimore and Ohio Rail Road, from which point the distance is 201 miles to Baltimore.

Petersburg is a small town on the South Branch; has an intelligent population, churches, and schools.

The Washington and Ohio Rail Road will enter this county from Hardy; and, passing through it, run into Tucker County, on the west. Grant County is expected to subscribe $100,000 to the capital stock of the Washington and Ohio Rail Road Company.

PENDLETON COUNTY, W. VA.,

Lies on the eastern line of the State, and adjoins the rich county of Rockingham, in the Valley of Virginia. Its area is 620 square miles. It is intersected by the south branch of the Potomac River and two affluents of the same, called the north and south forks, and by head branches of the James. The level of arable land from whence flow these streams, it is estimated, exceeds 2000 feet above the ocean.

Pendleton County was formed in 1788, and received its name from Edmund Pendleton, President of the Virginia Convention in 1775.

Although quite rugged and mountainous, this county is exceedingly•productive. Well-cultivated and highly improved farms are seen on the highest levels. The soil is fertile and the pasturage rich. It has an area of about 423,000 acres, one-fifth of which is under cultivation.

Pendleton ranks high as a stock-raising region, and in the production of grain, and there are annually produced large quantities of maple sugar.

During the summer months cattle are often driven from the southern portions of the State to the mountain regions of Pendleton, where, being freed from flies, they are found to thrive greatly.

The mountain lands, where not cleared, are generally in a state of nature, being covered with the original growth of timber. The prevailing kinds are oak, ash, hickory, sugar-maple, cherry, walnut, locust, chestnut, white pine, poplar, linn, and hemlock. Much of this timber is very superior, and suitable for ship and bridge building.

There are Pennsylvania-German settlements in several portions of the county.

Franklin is the county seat. It is an old-settled town, pleasantly situated on the south branch of the Potomac, 42 miles south of Moorefield, the county seat of Hardy, about 40 miles west of Harrisonburg, the seat of Rockingham County (and present terminus of the Manassas branch of the Orange, Alexandria, and Manassas Rail Road), and 35 or 40 miles from the Chesapeake and Ohio Rail Road, at its Buffalo Gap station. Franklin contains about 300 inhabitants. The usual county buildings are located here; there are churches and schools, and the people are kind and hospitable.

There is a very fine body of iron ore about three miles east of Franklin; it occurs in quantity. The ore is a very good hematite, and is famous throughout this region as that from which a horseshoe was forged; this shoe was sent to Richmond and placed in the State Cabinet.

There is a remarkably good water-power about three miles below Franklin, which is supplied by the Black Thorn branch, a bold and never-failing stream. A good brick merchant mill is always in operation here.

The waters of Buffalo Run have a fall of twenty to twenty-five feet; supply ample and permanent. This county is abundantly supplied with water-power for extensive manufacturing purposes.

The population of Pendleton County, according to the census of 1870, is 6455, and has nine post-offices.

Should the Washington and Ohio Rail Road not tap this county, it will nevertheless receive beneficial results from its passage through the adjoining counties of Hardy and Grant, with which it has communication by means of a fine road along the South Branch Valley.

Notwithstanding their remoteness from market, the lands along the VALLEY of the South Branch are high, ranging from twenty dollars per acre and upwards; but on the mountain ranges there are good farming lands, splendidly timbered, which can be purchased at from one dollar to ten dollars per acre, and in some cases for fifty cents per acre.

Most of the counties already mentioned lie in what is termed the " Valley Group," concerning which it is said, " For the variety and fertility of its soils, fine water-power, central position, salubrious and delightful climate, beauty and grandeur of scenery in plain and on mountain, it can literally and with severity of truth be said to be unsurpassed, if equalled, in the United States, or as a farming region in which to make homes of comfort, opulence, and refinement." A subscription of $56,000 to the stock of the Washington and Ohio Rail Road Company is expected from Pendleton County.

TUCKER COUNTY, W. VA.,

Adjoins Grant County on the west; is sparsely settled, the census of 1870 showing a population of 1907. It is divided into three townships, called Black Fork, Hannahsville, and Saint George, and has seven post-offices; is drained by Cheat River and its branches, which flows through it. Its mountains are the Alleghany, Cheat, and Laurel Hill. Although there is much mountain land in this county, it is varied with rolling upland and table land of excellent quality. The valleys are generally narrow, but fertile. Lands are very cheap, and can be purchased at rates largely below their intrinsic value.

The products of Tucker County are wheat, rye, corn, oats, potatoes, maple sugar, molasses, and honey. Juicy grasses abound, and large numbers of cattle are raised. Good pasturage is afforded almost to the summit of the mountains, and the valleys produce excellent corn and wheat. There is a fine region of country on the branches of Black Water, known as Canaan, a wilderness, but level and of great fertility, and covered with the heaviest forests. Coal is found on Red Creek, in this county, which, rising near the summit of the Alleghanies, flows westwardly into Cheat River or rather Dry Fork. This coal, $172\frac{3}{4}$ miles from tide-water at Alexandria, is the southern outcrop of the detached deposit to which the celebrated George's Creek coal belongs.

The Cambria County, Pennsylvania, iron ore beds, so extensively worked at Johnstown, in that State, are believed to extend into this county in the vicinity and south of St. George's.

SAINT GEORGE'S is the county town, about twenty-five miles from Rowlesburg station, Baltimore and Ohio Rail Road *via* Cheat River Valley.

Leaving Grant County the line of the Washington and Ohio Rail Road enters Tucker County on its southern border, and, passing through it westwardly, enters Randolph County.

A subscription of twenty-five thousand dollars to the stock of the Washington and Ohio Rail Road Company is expected from this county.

RANDOLPH COUNTY, W. VA.,

Lies west of Pendleton, and south of Tucker and Barbour, all of which counties it adjoins.

This county was formed in 1787, from Harrison, which was created three years earlier. Within its limits are several parallel ranges of mountains, with their intervening valleys. It is drained by Tygart's Valley River, Cheat River, and their numerous tributaries. On these streams are large tracts of timbered and arable lands. Much of the soil of the mountains is rich, and it abounds in slate, freestone, limestone, coal, and iron ore, and salt springs are numerous.

Randolph is a heavily wooded county. It has large areas of wild cherry and black walnut, and in such abundance that farm fences are made of this valuable timber, and large quantities are burned in order to clear the land. It has an unusual proportion of rich valley and smooth upland, the Main Cheat and Shaver's Mountains being the only rough ridges. The bottom land on Tygart's Valley River is very valuable. It is also a fine stock-raising region. Live stock of every description is annually exported to the eastern markets. The farms are generally well improved, and new farms can be opened at very small cost.

In it there is a very superior coal for making gas, at a distance of 102 miles nearer to navigation, *via* the Washington and Ohio Rail Road, than the gas coal which is so extensively carried upon the Baltimore and Ohio Rail Road. The distance by the Washington and Ohio Rail Road to the Cumberland coal is thirty-six miles less than by the Baltimore and Ohio Rail Road. This saving of distance, and consequently of time and cost of transportation (of such an article as coal), will, *of itself*, secure to the Washington and Ohio Rail Road an unlimited and very profitable business.

Jonathan M. Bennett, Esq., for many years the auditor of the State of Virginia, and familiar with the route of the Washington and Ohio Rail Road through West Virginia, says:— ·

"On the Buckhannon River, in Randolph County, there is land having on it not less than thirty to forty poplar trees to the acre, thirty of which will measure 80 to 100 feet each to the first limb, 'straight as a gun-barrel,' and 5 feet through at the butt. At other points, where cherry trees preponderate, an acre can be selected having on it twenty trees which will measure 50 feet to the first limb, perfectly straight, and 3 feet through the butt. A group of sugar maples can be shown, in a single cove in the mountains, having on it not less than five thousand trees. In 1869, in passing through these woods, I crossed a poplar tree that had been cut down, and from curiosity measured it, and found it was 85 feet to the first limb, and 6 feet across the stump at the narrowest part, and 6 feet 2 inches at the widest, and it was by no means the largest in the group; and whilst I did not measure it to ascertain the fact, it was apparently as thick at the first limb as at the butt."

In the summer of 1869, Professor McFadden, of the University of Ohio, passed over the line of the Washington and Ohio Rail Road, and from his letters to a gentleman in the State of Delaware, the following, relating to Randolph County, is extracted:—

"Rich Mountain, *that* next west of the Alleghany, between the Dry Fork and Laurel Fork of Cheat River, is rightly named from the fertility of the soil. The greater part of it could be brought under cultivation. It is now covered with a very dense and heavy forest of maple, oak, ash, walnut, poplar, etc. The trees are generally large, and mostly free from an undergrowth of laurel. The walnut and poplar trees are not very numerous, but some are very large and valuable. This whole region will be very valuable for its timber and for farming when it is made accessible by means of the Washington and Ohio Rail Road. It has a capacity for supporting a dense population. The building of a railroad through the valley of any branch of Cheat River will increase the present value of lands from three to twenty fold.

"These lands are used for the purpose of summer grazing cattle, and the whole region seems peculiarly adapted to the growth of grass. The climate is cool and moist, which, in connection with

6

some peculiarity of the soil, produces a luxuriant growth of rich and nutritious grass. The region is also abundantly supplied with springs of cool and never-failing water. Cattle do remarkably well, and the milk is certainly the richest and best I ever saw. The country on the head waters of Cheat River is destined to be a famous dairy region. On the southern end of Rich Mountain, there is land from which the timber was cleared in the spring of 1868, and which produced good grass the same year, and the following year mowed a heavy crop of clover and timothy without stirring the soil or sowing a seed."

Randolph County is divided into nine townships; contains, according to the census of 1870, a population of 5563, and has nine post-offices.

Immigration is much needed, and a cordial welcome extended to all.

Beverly, the county seat of Randolph, contains the usual county buildings, churches, and schools. It lies on a handsome plain, near Tygart's Valley River, and has about 500 inhabitants; is centrally located in one of the wildest parts of Tygart's Valley; is fifty miles from Clarksburg, an important town in Harrison County, forty-four miles to Webster Station, Baltimore and Ohio Rail Road, and, by Staunton turnpike, seventy-nine miles to Buffalo Gap, Chesapeake and Ohio Rail Road.

Mr. James M. Brown, a practical English miner, examined the coal lands of this county, and his letter of December 5, 1872, is herewith published.

The Washington and Ohio Railroad enters this county from Tucker, and passes through it into Upshur, along the southern border of Barbour County. A subscription of $50,000 is expected from this county to the capital stock of the Washington and Ohio Rail Road Company.

BARBOUR COUNTY, W. VA.,

Was formed in 1843, and named from the distinguished Virginia family of that name. It lies west of Tucker County, from which it is separated by Laurel Mountain. It is 30 miles long and 15 wide. The eastern part is mountainous, the western hilly. Much of the soil is fertile and adapted to grazing. It is drained by Tygart's Valley River and its tributaries. So far as improved, this county is prolific in crops of corn and in cattle, and with the facilities it will receive from the passage through it of the Washington and Ohio Rail Road its growth will be substantial and rapid. At the heads of Simpson's and Elk Creeks, and on the Buckhannon and Tygart's Valley Rivers it is thickly settled. Barbour County contains many well improved farms: coal and iron in abundance. The county is divided into seven townships, has eleven post-offices, and 10,312 population.

PHILIPPI COURT HOUSE, the county seat, is twenty miles southeast from Clarksburg, Harrison county, and fourteen miles from Webster Station on the Baltimore and Ohio Rail Road, 283 miles from Baltimore. It enjoys a favorable location in a fertile country on the east side of Tygart's Valley River. It is in Philippi township, which contains a population of 1605. In this vicinity there is an abundance of coal and iron ore of an excellent quality.

The Washington and Ohio Rail Road crosses this county on its southern boundary, and will develop coal lands of great value.

UPSHUR COUNTY, W. VA.,

Joins Barbour and Harrison on the north, Lewis County on the west, and Randolph on the east. It is watered by Buckhannon River, a fork of Tygart's Valley River, and the head branches of Elk River. This county forms the first bench on the gradual ascent toward the mountains, the Buckhannon Fork level being probably 250 feet above the head valleys of Elk Creek and Stone Coal Creek immediately adjacent. Diversified surface, in part rough, with a fair proportion rich, undulating, and gently sloping, embracing some fine grazing table lands towards head waters. It contains a number of well improved and productive farms, and of bituminous and cannel coals and iron ore there are vast quantities.

Jonathan M. Bennett, Esq., before quoted, says: "There is a vein of coal on Buckhannon River which is said to be twelve feet thick, and I do not doubt it;" and Col. R. L. Brown, formerly a member of the Virginia Legislature from this county, in a late letter says: "Speaking of coal fires suggests to me that I never really enjoyed them except in this country. I have two coal banks developed within 300 yards of my dwelling; supply inexhaustible. I pay one cent a bushel for digging, and haul it myself, so that the coal I consume costs but one cent per bushel. My thirty-inch grate burns out two and a half bushels in twenty-four hours, but I run it steadily night and day. When I throw the coal on I never think about burning money."

Upshur is a fine cattle county, and produces abundantly of wheat, corn, oats, tobacco, potatoes, etc.

Buckhannon is the county seat. It is well located twenty-eight miles rom Clarksburg by turnpike, has one newspaper, and contains 475 inhabitants. The usual county buildings are located here, also schools and churches.

According to the census of 1870 the county contained a population of 8498. The people are kind and hospitable, and immigration is greatly desired. Lands are cheap. Some well improved farms can be purchased at from ten to fifteen and twenty dollars per acre, and good farming lands without improvements at one to three dollars per acre.

The Washington and Ohio Rail Road enters this county from Barbour, and crosses the Buckhannon River at the town of Buckhannon, two hundred and twenty-four and three-fourths miles from Alexandria, into the county of Lewis.

The county of Upshur has already subscribed one hundred thousand dollars to the capital stock of the Washington and Ohio Rail Road Company, said subscription to be available on the road reaching its county limits.

BRAXTON COUNTY, W. VA.,

Lies west of and adjoining the counties of Lewis, Webster, and Upshur. It was formed in 1836, and received its name from Carter Braxton, one of the signers of the Declaration of American Independence. It is drained by the Little Kanawha and Elk Rivers and their branches.

The country is generally rough, but fertile and well watered, and contains a good proportion of smooth upland. Like the other counties in the State of West Virginia, Braxton contains a considerable quantity of fine timbered lands which are underlaid with coal and iron. Its springs are valuable for their medicinal properties, and with the facilities it will enjoy by means of the Washington and Ohio Rail Road, these will attract the health-seeking from the Atlantic Coast and the Ohio and Mississippi Valleys. About one-eighth of its productive lands are under cultivation, from which good crops of wheat, corn, oats, potatoes, tobacco, etc., are obtained. Its grass lands are capable of supporting large numbers of sheep and cattle, and the railroad will give renewed energy to this branch of industry. The manufacture of salt received attention to some extent at Bulltown, in this county, prior to the war. But the great need of the county is immigration and capital, and these ought to be attracted by the advantages it possesses. It has a fine climate, abundant water-power for manufacturing and other purposes, a kind and industrious population, and the immigrant is sure to meet a cordial welcome.

Lands can be purchased at low figures, improved farming lands at five to fifteen dollars per acre, and unimproved from two to five dollars per acre.

Braxton County has eight post-offices, which are regularly and promptly served. Population 6480.

SUTTON, the county seat of Braxton, is accessible from Clarksburg, *via* Weston, Lewis Co., sixty miles from the Baltimore and Ohio Rail Road on the north, and ninety miles from the Chesapeake and Ohio Rail Road on the south.

The Washington and Ohio Rail Road, occupying a central position between these, will drain the country for many miles on either side of its line, and afford to Braxton County the means of increasing its productions and wealth.

WEBSTER COUNTY, W. VA.,

Joins Braxton, Upshur, and Randolph on the north and west; is drained by the head-waters of the Elk and Gauley Rivers, and possesses excellent pasturage. It is sparsely settled, and but little cultivated. Its lands are cheap, and offer fine opportunities to parties engaged in the raising of stock.

Webster County is crossed from east to west by a number of narrow parallel valleys, separated by high ridges, which impede communication in a north and south direction. Good roads would make this an attractive country.

This county is well supplied with deposits of bituminous coal, and shows many indications of iron ore. Salt was formerly manufactured in Webster, and, with capital, could be produced in paying quantity.

Webster is divided into three townships, viz., Fork Lick, Glade, and Holly; contains 1730 in population, and has eight post-offices.

Its uplands and table-lands of good surface and soil, in large tracts, can be purchased at from fifty cents to one dollar and a half per acre. Unimproved farms in the valleys at from $5 to $10 per acre.

Addison is the county seat (the post-office address is Webster C. H.), thirty miles from Sutton, the court-house of Braxton County.

This county, although not touched by the Washington and Ohio Rail Road, is tributary to it, and will receive great benefit from its passage through the adjoining counties.

LEWIS COUNTY, W. VA.,

Is bounded on the north by Harrison and Doddridge, west by Gilmer, south by Braxton, and east by Upshur County. Is watered by the west fork of the Monongahela River and its numerous tributaries. Surface hilly and rolling, and uniformly fertile. The character of its lands is very fine for farming purposes. Its productions are wheat, Indian corn, oats, tobacco, potatoes, hay, etc. It ranks high as a stock raising district, having ample pasturage, grazes many thousand head of cattle, and is a very thriving county. The farms are well improved, and, as in the counties east and west of it, the people are anxious for intelligent immigration. The population of this county in 1870, according to the United States census, was 11,286.

Lewis County is abundantly supplied with water power for manufacturing purposes. It contains vast tracts of the finest timber, and is underlaid with beds of coal, iron, and other minerals. By means of the facilities shortly to be afforded by the Washington and Ohio Rail Road, these must be productive of great wealth to the country. This county presents a fine field to the enterprising man with capital, with the certainty of liberal returns for the means and labor expended.

WESTON, the county seat of Lewis, contains a population of about 1200. Is a well located and growing town, containing much solid wealth. The West Virginia " Hospital for the Insane," a large and first class structure, is located here. One newspaper, the " Weston Democrat," is published here.

Passing through Upshur, the Washington and Ohio Rail Road enters Lewis, and runs through the county at or near Weston to Gilmer County.

Lewis County is expected to subscribe two hundred thousand dollars to the stock of the Washington and Ohio Rail Road Company.

HARRISON COUNTY, W. VA.,

Was created in 1784, and named in honor of Benjamin Harrison, Governor of Virginia from 1781 to 1784, and father of General William Henry Harrison, late President of the United States.

Harrison is north of Lewis and Upshur, and binds Taylor and Barbour Counties on the east. Is finely watered by the west fork of the Monongahela River and its tributary streams. The surface is rolling and hilly, with expansive valleys. The soil is rich, the county containing many highly improved farms. The timber is very fine, and water power abundant; large seams of bituminous coal, already developed; also, cannel coal and iron ore. Salt was formerly manufactured at Clarksburg. The Baltimore and Ohio Rail Road passes through the centre of this county, in which it has several stations.

CLARKSBURG, the county seat, on the Baltimore and Ohio Rail Road, is three hundred and one miles from Baltimore, and eighty-two from Parkersburg; contains about 1500 inhabitants, the usual county buildings, churches, and schools; is beautifully located on a plateau at the junction of Elk Creek and the west fork of the Monongahela River, and enjoys the advantages derived from much solid wealth and unsurpassed natural elements of growth and prosperity which are, as yet, but partially developed; has a bank with a capital of $100,000, two newspapers, and the United States District Court for West Virginia holds its sessions here.

The population of Harrison County is 16,714, as shown by the census of 1870.

The Washington and Ohio Rail Road runs near the southern line of Harrison County, and will open that part of the county which receives little, if any, advantage from the Baltimore and Ohio Rail Road.

DODDRIDGE COUNTY, W. VA.,

Adjoins Harrison and Lewis Counties on the west; is watered by Middle Island Creek and Hughes' River and branches; surface is rolling and hilly; good soil and valuable timber; is a pastoral and grain-producing section; contains 7076 inhabitants; is traversed by the northwestern and other turnpikes. The Baltimore and Ohio Rail Road has six stations in this county. Its passage is through the northern portion of the county.

The county town of Doddridge is West Union, a station on the Baltimore and Ohio Rail Road, containing 600 inhabitants, fifty-five and a half miles from Parkersburg, and three hundred and twenty-seven from Baltimore.

Saint Clair Colony, a German settlement, is fifteen miles south of West Union, on Cove Creek.

The passage of the Washington and Ohio Rail Road, through the adjoining counties of Lewis and Gilmer, will give to parties residing along the southern border of Doddridge good railroad facilities, and, being much shorter to tide-water than the existing routes, will contribute to the wealth and importance of the county.

GILMER COUNTY, W. VA.,

Lies west of Lewis and Braxton, which counties it adjoins. Is watered by the Little Kanawha River, Steer, Cedar, and Leading Creeks, and by numerous other streams. The soil is rich; surface generally rolling and hilly, with some fine bottom lands. Gilmer abounds in timber, coal, and iron, and has fine and abundant water power for manufacturing purposes, and is well adapted to grazing. Its productions are wheat, corn, oats, tobacco, potatoes, etc., and stock in considerable quantity. Is divided into four townships, contains 4512 inhabitants, and has nine post offices.

In this county from 75,000 to 80,000 acres of uncultivated land can be obtained in a single tract, at a low price, for the settlement of immigrants, who can enjoy the unrivalled advantages of municipal government, worshipping at their own altar, and educating their children in their own way.

Glenville is the county seat, containing a population of 300. Is 75 miles from Point Pleasant, 250 from Washington, D. C., 40 from Spencer, Roane County, and 33 miles from the Baltimore and Ohio Rail Road at West Union Station. Glenville is in the township of that name, which contains 1422 inhabitants.

Leaving the western limit of Lewis County the Washington and Ohio Rail Road enters Gilmer, and passing through it by Glenville, runs into Calhoun County.

Gilmer County has subscribed $75,000 to the stock of the Washington and Ohio Rail Road Company, which will become available on the road reaching the limits of the county.

CALHOUN COUNTY, W. VA.,

Lies west of Gilmer and Braxton; the Little Kanawha, its west fork and Steer Creek are the principal streams.

This county covers a small extent of territory, and is devoted principally to the raising of stock. Its lands are rich, hilly, and rolling, and its productions of wheat, corn, oats, tobacco, etc., are considerable; contains fine timbered tracts, good water-powers, and the capacity for sustaining a considerable population.

Is divided into five townships, has six post-offices, and contains a population of 2961, who enjoy the advantages of churches and schools.

Improved lands can be purchased at $5 to $15 per acre, and lands unimproved at $2 to $5 per acre. Large timbered tracts at less prices.

Grantsville is the county seat. Is accessible from the Baltimore and Ohio Rail Road, via Ellenboro Station, 386 miles from Baltimore.

The Washington and Ohio Rail Road enters Calhoun from Gilmer, and passes into Roane County.

Like Gilmer, this county can furnish large bodies of land in one of the most healthy countries on the globe, for settlement in large colonies, where they can enjoy their own municipal government and freedom in religious opinions.

Calhoun County has made a subscription of fifty thousand dollars to the stock of the Washington and Ohio Rail Road Company, which will become available on the road reaching its border.

ROANE COUNTY, W. VA.,

Received its name from the eminent Virginia family of that name. Is situated on the west boundary of Calhoun. Wirt County lies on its north line, and Jackson binds it on the west. Is abundantly watered by Reedy Creek, Spring Creek, west fork of Little Kanawha River, and the head branches of Pocatalico River.

This is a picturesque region, "full of wooded hills and grassy dales." Sheep, cattle, and horses are largely produced in this county, and besides the cereals tobacco and fruit are extensively as well as profitably cultivated.

The surface is hilly, with some considerable valleys and low flat hills in the southern portion of the county, and nearly all of it exceedingly rich.

This is also a fine timbered region. Lands cheap, and immigration desired. Unimproved lands with elegant timber can be purchased at prices ranging from $2 to $5 per acre. Improved lands from $7 to $15 per acre. Coal and iron ore abound in this county, and with the passage through Roane of the Washington and Ohio Rail Road, its lands will advance tenfold over present prices. Roane County contains 7375 inhabitants; twenty years ago it had but three settlers. Is divided into seven townships, has eight post-offices, county roads, schools, and churches.

Spencer (C. H.) is the county seat, contains a population of about

200. Is pleasantly situated in Spring Creek Valley, 20 miles from Little Kanawha River, and 35 miles from Ravenswood Landing (Jackson County on the Ohio River.

From Calhoun the route of the Washington and Ohio Rail Road is through Roane, near California, into Jackson County.

A subscription of seventy-five thousand dollars to the capital stock of the Washington and Ohio Rail Road Company is expected from this county.

WIRT COUNTY, W. VA.,

Lies on the northern boundaries of Calhoun, Roane, and Jackson Counties. Is drained by the Little Kanawha River and its west fork, Spring, Reedy and Tucker Creeks.

The surface is hilly and rolling, with fine valley lands on the river and creeks. The soil is rich and well adapted to grazing and farming purposes. Its cereal productions are large, but it is principally noted for the oil belt which extends through the county. The oil region "about Wirt Court House" is one of the richest in the country, and is known as the "ETERNAL CENTRE," a well not being considered *good* that does not yield 300 barrels a day. These wells are numerous, and are capable of furnishing freight sufficient for the support of a railroad. For want of better transportation, these oils at present reach the seaboard by means of the Little Kanawha River to Parkersburg, Wood County, thence by Baltimore and Ohio Rail Road to Baltimore, 384 miles distant. With the completion of the Washington and Ohio Rail Road, this valuable product will reach Alexandria and tidewater at a saving of about 70 miles in cost of transportation, a very important item to parties engaged in the development of this branch of industry.

Wirt County is divided into seven townships, contains 4804 inhabitants, and has nine post-offices; at one of these, "Burning Springs," there is a telegraph line to Parkersburg.

Elizabeth is the county town (post-office address Wirt C. H.), a pleasantly located and active village, twenty-two miles from Parkersburg, and ten miles from Walker's Station, Baltimore and Ohio Rail Road, from which point Baltimore is distant by rail 369 miles.

JACKSON COUNTY, W. VA.,

Was formed in 1831 from parts of Mason, Kanawha, and Wood Counties. Its length is thirty-three miles, and its mean breadth twenty-four miles. Is bounded by the Ohio River on the west, and by Wirt and Roane Counties on the east.

Is watered by the Ohio River, Big Mill Creek, and numerous other streams. The surface is hilly and rolling. Soils good, portions of which are limestone. Good sized bottoms on all the principal streams, the soils of which are of the first quality. Its products are corn, wheat, maple syrup in large quantities, honey, butter, potatoes, fruit, and tobacco. It is a good timber and coal region, and large numbers of cattle are bred and grazed in it.

Its principal landings on the Ohio River are Ravenswood and Ripley Landings.

It is divided into five townships, and contains 10,888 inhabitants.

Ripley, twelve miles from the Ohio River, is the court house or county seat, contains 300 inhabitants, and is situated in Mill Creek township, which has a population of 2821. The county town is a small but active place, and has two newspapers, the usual county buildings, with churches and schools. The county has sixteen post-offices.

The Washington and Ohio Rail Road enters this county from Roane, and, passing through it from east to west, runs into Mason County.

A subscription of $100,000 to the stock of the Washington and Ohio Rail Road Company is expected from this county.

MASON COUNTY, W. VA.,

Was formed in 1804, from Kanawha County, and received its name from the celebrated statesman, George Mason, the framer of the first constitution of Virginia, the author of the first Bill of Rights, and a member of the convention which framed the constitution of the United States.

Mason County is about 30 miles long, 22 broad, and has an area of 300 square miles. The Ohio River forms its western boundary, the counties of Jackson and Putnam join it on the east and south, and the Great Kanawha River passes centrally through it. It has numerous other streams. Is a wealthy county, is intersected by turnpikes and county roads, and enjoys the advantages of several landings on its 80 miles of river front. It has one hundred miles of bottom lands of unsurpassed fertility, and is becoming, from its resources and its advantageous situation, a very thriving portion of the State. This county presents an inviting area of fine farming lands. Is well adapted to the cereals, and produces heavy crops of wheat, corn, oats, etc. Is a fine stock raising region, of which its exportations are very large. Has fine timber, which is underlaid with large bodies of coal and iron ore. The manufacture of salt is conducted on an extensive scale, and this business can and ought to be largely increased.

The population of Mason County is 20,811, among which will be found immigrants from the States of Pennsylvania, Ohio, Maryland, Kentucky, and New York, and from England, Ireland, Scotland, and other foreign States. It has 19 post-offices, and is divided into 10 townships.

Mason County contains several important villages or towns; of these, Hartford has 918 inhabitants, New Haven 489, Point Pleasant 773, Clifton 693, Mason 1182, and West Columbia 778.

Several newspapers are published in the county.

POINT PLEASANT, the county-seat, is situated at the mouth of the Kanawha River, one of the most advantageous locations on the Ohio. It has two newspapers and a bank with a large capital, and, being the western terminus of the Washington and Ohio Rail Road, will become on its completion *the* great point, at the west, for receiving and shipping supplies eastward and westward.

DISTANCES ON THE OHIO.

From Point Pleasant to Huntington, the western terminus of the Chesapeake and Ohio Rail Road, it is 37 miles, and from Point Pleasant to Parkersburg and Wheeling, the termini of the Baltimore and Ohio Rail Road, it is 76 and 170 miles, respectively.

A subscription of two hundred and fifty thousand dollars to the capital stock of the Washington and Ohio Rail Road Company is expected from Mason County, to become available on the road reaching the limits of the county.

The Washington and Ohio Rail Road is not equalled in shortness by any other work already completed, in progress or contemplated, nor is it *necessarily* in antagonism to any other work.

This, and many more trunk roads from the Ohio to the Atlantic waters, are absolute public necessities for transportation across the portage between the rivers of the great valley and the eastern seaboard; they are as indispensable to the life and growth and health of the country as arteries are to the human body.

This great valley between the Alleghanies and the Rocky Mountains contains five-eighths, or more, of the sources of production and wealth of the United States.

These resources are, as yet, only in the beginning of their development, and that on no more than a fragment of their surface.

If so vast in their infancy, what will their maturity be—and who can conjecture any limit to their development?

The present and future productions of this region, of value and extent so utterly incalculable, must seek the Atlantic coast for access to the wants and to the markets of the Eastern United States, of Europe, and of the Old World, from whence too it must draw the supplies it needs from them in exchange. The current of commerce *must* be eastward, with a reflex stream.

Its people, too, must travel eastward in the direction of their commercial interests, and the streams of travel to and fro, between the great valley and the eastern border, immense already, must increase in geometrical progression.

For all this, transportation is needful. This transportation, for its people and products, the valley *must* and *will* have; it is becoming, with its people, *the living and great question of the day.* The supply of the means of shipment and travel is the limit and measure of their growth and prosperity.

Let any one take the statistics of surface and of the present production, trade, and travel, and let him calculate the tonnage of freight *now* to be moved, and the number of persons *now* to be carried *each way.* Let him reckon up the number of cars needed, and the time required between the Ohio, or the Lakes, and the sea-board; and he will see that the lines *now* in operation, or contemplated, are totally inadequate to the wants of the *present even.* Let him then consider the increase of population, trade, and travel, always accruing from every addition to the facilities of communication, add also the *local* interests and business developed on the lines of each road, and the inquirer will see that there is work for every line now built or contemplated, to its utmost capacity, and for five times more.

So far from this, or any other roads which connect the sea and the Ohio, injuring each other, they help each other by multiplying (as roads with *such termini* always do), the general demand for communication.

If a railroad be built through a region which, before that, was amply accommodated by a tri-weekly stage for travel, and by farm wagons for freight—in the first year of its operation, the *minimum* daily freight and travel, over the railroad, will be many hundred per cent. over the maximum of the days before it was built.

It is a law, as certain as those of nature, that every work of the kind *creates,* as well as supplies, the demand for it, and, if the area for this multiplication be sufficient, the road must prosper. The great valley furnishes this area of increase. ample for all the roads built and contemplated.

There are now *but ten* through lines of transportation built or contemplated between the waters of the valley and the tide waters of the Atlantic.

1. The route by the Great Lakes, and through Canada to the St. Lawrence.

2. The Erie Canal, in New York. from Lake Erie, at Buffalo, to the city of New York, *via* the Hudson River.

3. The New York Central Rail Road, touching the western waters, on Lake Erie at Buffalo.

4. The New York and Erie Rail Road, terminating on Lake Erie, at Dunkirk.

5. The Sunbury and Erie Rail Road, and connections, from Erie; Pennsylvania. on Lake Erie, to the Delaware, at Philadelphia.

6. The Pennsylvania Central Rail Road, from the Ohio at Pittsburg to the Delaware at Philadelphia.

7. The Baltimore and Ohio Rail Road, from the Ohio, at Wheeling and Parkersburg, to the arm of the Chesapeake Bay at Baltimore.

8. The Washington and Ohio Rail Road, from the Ohio at Point Pleasant to the Potomac tide-water at Alexandria and Washington Cities.

9. The Chesapeake and Ohio Rail Road, from the Ohio at Huntington to the James River at Richmond, and, *via* Rail or James River, to the Bay at Norfolk.

10. South of these, may be mentioned the Memphis and Charleston Rail Road, which has indirect connection with the great west from the Mississippi, at Memphis, to the city of Charleston, South Carolina, on the Ashley and Cooper Rivers.

Of these, 5 *only*, the Pennsylvania Central Rail Road. the Baltimore and Ohio Rail Road, the Washington and Ohio Rail Road, the

Chesapeake and Ohio Rail Road, and the Memphis and Charleston Rail Road, can be accessible and operative for western freight, *all the year round.*

The other 5 are inaccessible, from the West, by water, or are suspended entirely during 4 or 5 months of ice and frost.

So that there are but 5 outlets, *now* built, or in progress, by which the freight of the great valley can have *continuous*, sure, and certain transportation during each of the 365 days of the year, and *the Washington and Ohio Rail Road is one of these five.*

The Pennsylvania Central, the Baltimore and Ohio, the Chesapeake and Ohio, and the Memphis and Charleston are the only ones *now* in operation of the last named five, and their full capacity is taxed to its utmost, and is insufficient for their local trade, and for the pressure of the trade of the west.

Of the three and a half millions (in round numbers) of square miles in the United States, at least two millions lie between the Alleghany and the Rocky Mountains.

Of the thirty-eight and a half millions of population, about seventeen millions live in this valley, and the average increase of population in the States and Territories therein, in ten years, has ranged from 9 per cent. in some, to 520 per cent. in others.

This whole region has *continuous and perpetual water* (as well as railway) communication with the Virginia side of the Ohio River, and at *this* Virginia shore the water lines of the valley approach the tides of the Atlantic *more nearly than at any other point on the continent,* the distance from Point Pleasant, the western terminus of the Washington and Ohio Rail Road, to the tide-water of the Potomac, at Alexandria, being *only 325 miles,* or twenty-four hours portage of freight

Point Pleasant, on the Ohio, is *always* accessible to steamers and barges without interruption from low water, while from Alexandria, its eastern port, with a depth of water great enough for men-of-war, there is an open way to the ocean, rarely closed by ice, and then only for a very few days in the year.

Western freight *must* seek that route which is the most certain and cheap—which involves the shortest amount of railroad carriage.

Hence it *must* concentrate on the short portage of but a single day from water to water across the States of Virginia and West Virginia, by the Virginia roads, no matter what may be its ultimate destination.

It must get from water to water as quickly and cheaply as may be.

Can it be said that any one or two roads can satisfy this demand, or supply these wants?

From these data it can be mathematically demonstrated that when the Washington and Ohio Rail Road is completed to the Ohio River, connecting with the nine hundred and odd navigable miles of that river, and through it with the network of navigable waters of the great valley, as well as with its railways, and becomes the *shortest and easiest of all portages* between these western waters and the ocean, it will be sure of profitable employment to the outside limit of the capacity of any first-class road.

A torrent of trade and travel, *now* dammed up in the west for want of adequate and cheap transportation, will rush over the Washington and Ohio Rail Road, and over any other road on this short portage seeking the shortest, surest, and cheapest route to the sea.

It will be like cutting the dykes, like a crevasse in the levee, like tapping the furnace, and the flood will well nigh overwhelm the cities at the eastern terminus.

Nor let it be forgotten that the line of this road passes through eighteen of the best counties in Virginia and West Virginia, traverses in many of them inexhaustible deposits of coal and iron, and other minerals of commerce, opens up vast tracts of the finest timber in the Union, besides giving a market to the grazing and grain farms along the whole 325 miles of its line. Add its local and home trade to the western demand, count up the natural increment of both, and what doubt can remain that this, the shortest, cheapest, and easiest transit from water to water will be one of the most successful and paying roads in the land?

With but ten bars to the gridiron at any time, with but five of these effective at all times, any one can see how inadequate are the present means of transportation, how greatly this inadequacy checks production, how the deficiency retards and dwarfs the growth of the west, and how, without their completion, the coal and iron on the lines contemplated must continue to repose in the sleep which has been undisturbed since the creation, the silence must be unbroken by the sound of the factory, and the water-power flow on in the waste which has continued for centuries.

Any one can see that the lines now in operation are inadequate to meet the increasing wants, and *that this road and more* are needed.

There is enough employment for all and more in the great work of multiplying and moving the productions and supplies of the valley, in meeting that demand for short, cheap, and uninterrupted transit which is ringing throughout the west, the need of which is hourly pressing upon them, and in a measure paralyzing their energies.

85

For additional information as to the value of the country traversed by the Washington and Ohio Rail Road, attention is called to the letters of J. M. Bennett, Esq., a Senator of West Virginia, and James M. Brown, Esq., of the State of Pennsylvania. The latter gentleman, a practical English miner, has recently returned from an inspection of the counties of Randolph and Barbour.

STATE OF WEST VIRGINIA,
SENATE CHAMBER, CHARLESTON, November 25, 1872.

HON. L. McKENZIE,
President Washington and Ohio Rail Road, Alexandria, Va.

DEAR SIR: Your letter of the 7th instant was received just as I left home to take my seat here as a Senator of West Virginia, and I have postponed answering it in order that I might the better inform myself as to the inquiries you made.

The natural resources along the line of your road from Winchester to the Ohio River, in Mason County, are chiefly iron, limestone, coal, salt, timber, and water-powers.

The region from Winchester to the Alleghany Mountains constitutes a section of that great iron belt, which, commencing in New York, runs in a southwest direction, passing through Pennsylvania, furnishing many of the largest of the furnaces of that State with their stocks; crosses Maryland; enters Virginia with the Alleghanies, forming its eastern base and spurs throughout the whole breadth of the State, and extends on to the southwest. In this belt, though, ores, for the most part, are the oxides of iron, yielding in Virginia from forty to fifty per cent. of iron (hematite). In speaking of the Valley of Virginia, in which Winchester is situated, Prof. Rogers, in his State Geological Report of Virginia, says: "Of the twelve rocks, each marked by certain distinctive characters, composing the mountains and valleys of this region, it has been determined that at least eight are accompanied by beds of iron ore, many of which yield a metal of the finest quality;" while Gen. Haupt, Chief Engineer of the Shenandoah Valley Rail Road, in speaking of the minerals along the line of his road, which runs in this valley, says that "Pennsylvania, rich as she is, is poor in iron ores as compared with Virginia." Many of these ores have been worked and well proven in the small furnaces of this region, but they have never done a large business, both from want of transportation and because they had to look to charcoal as a fuel; and timber is too soon stripped from the immediate vicinity of a furnace to depend upon it as a smelting agent in very large works. For this latter reason,

7

therefore, these ores must look to other sources for their reduction, and most naturally will they turn to the West Virginia coal, as it is the nearest, as well as of the most excellent and superior quality for that purpose.

These iron ores, which, as I have said, yield from forty to fifty per cent. of iron, can be placed on the cars from lands contiguous to your road at from one dollar and twenty-five cents to two dollars per ton, or, if a furnace is on the property, at its tunnel head, at the same rate. The Lake Superior and Missouri ores cost, delivered in Pittsburg, thirteen dollars to fourteen dollars per ton.

" In Hampshire County," says Professor Rogers, in the report before referred to, " upon a stratum of valuable iron not less than fifteen feet thick, there rests a bed of sandstone, upon which reposes a coal seam three feet thick, above this another bed of sandstone, then a two-foot vein of coal, then sandstone, then another coal seam of four feet, again a stratum of sandstone, and over it a seven-foot vein of coal : over this a heavy bed of iron ore, and, crowning the series, an enormous coal seam of from fifteen feet to twenty feet in thickness."

In this region is limestone in plenty and of the best quality for use in the blast-furnace, while for lime and hydraulic cement some of it ranks very high.

From Hardy County, inclusive, your road runs in the great coal field of West Virginia.

What else is needed but the establishment of a railroad to bring this coal and iron together, and to take the manufactured products to market, to induce the establishment of large and extensive blast-furnaces, rolling-mills, machine-shops, etc.?

West of the Alleghanies is a country of simple geological structure, belonging to the coal measures. The strata dip with a slight and uniform angle towards the Valley of the Ohio; everything bespeaks it to have been at one time an expanded plain, which was gently tilted from the horizontal position. The form, direction, and character of both hills and valleys give evidence that its inequalities of surface were caused by the furrowing action of a mighty and devastating rush of waters, which, by rapid drainage, scooped out enormous valleys and basins in the upper strata, leaving most of the coal-bearing strata (which contain all the varieties of coal, save lignite and anthracite) above water-level, and making thousands of available points for the coal miner to begin operations; whilst the nearly horizontal position alluded to keeps whatever valuable minerals may be in the ground near the surface, or at an accessible depth, over enormously wide spaces of country.

The advantages mining will derive from this portion of the coal above water-level will be plainly seen by comparing this country and Great Britain in that respect. The cost of sinking shafts in the New-castle region of that country to one thousand feet has been, in many instances, one thousand dollars per yard.

In the great northern coal fields of England, producing twenty millions of tons of coal per annum, there are two hundred pits, costing, for first outlay for sinking and machinery, fifty millions of dollars, to which must be added the necessary expenses in main-taining air-courses, etc., requisite to the safety of the employees. There is now invested, simply in pits and machinery for pumping and hoisting the one hundred millions of tons of coal produced annually in Great Britain, two hundred million dollars, and this vast sum is destined to utter destruction in serving the purposes for which it is used.

In West Virginia the mighty natural forces to which I have referred have already sunk all necessary pits and shafts, which need neither repair nor renewal. The inclination of the strata, coupled with the laws of gravity, have provided the most costless, perfect, and permanent pumping machinery, and the perfect ventilation of the mines is but a matter of the most ordinary care.

Owing to the lack of communication with the outside world of the region through which the Washington and Ohio Rail Road passes, there have been heretofore no inducements to open up the various seams of coal, save at the foot of the hills, or where they may be most accessible to supply neighborhood demands, and, consequently, I am unable to give you details as to individual seams, or to state the thickness of the thickest; but I may state that the celebrated Pittsburg seam, which, at Clarksburg, in the adjoining county to Lewis, measures from ten to twelve feet, has been traced across the line of your road by Prof. Rogers; that to the north, in Preston County, seams of eight to ten feet have been proven, while in Clay and Nicholas Counties, to the south, eight, ten, and eleven-foot ones have been opened, though, for want of transportation, not yet worked.

This coal and iron on which I have thus dwelt constitute the mine-ral wealth of the country along the line of the Washington and Ohio Rail Road.

The world's demand for iron exceeds the supply; the prices of pig metal within the last twelve months have risen in England over one hundred per cent., and in this country have put the price up to fifty-six dollars. Therefore, on the market for iron I need say nothing, but allow me to call your attention to that for coal in the West.

By means of the Washington and Ohio Rail Road the coal along its line will be brought into communication with the great Mississippi Valley, and its 20,000 miles of navigable waters, and its system of 20,000 miles of railroad now in successful operation, and their hundreds and thousands of coal burning engines, locomotives, factories, furnaces, and machine shops.

These rivers and railroads wash the shores and traverse the country of sixteen magnificent, populous, and growing States, with an area of one million square miles, and minister to the wants of ten millions of people.

The better to form some idea of this mighty western country, I would state, on the authority of a pamphlet issued by Messrs. Fisk & Hatch, of New York, in the interest of the Chesapeake and Ohio Rail Road, " That the tonnage of the upper Ohio in steamers, barges, and boats exceeds that of New York ; and that of the Ohio, as estimated by government engineers, exceeds the entire foreign commerce of the United States."

The consumption of coal throughout the West was increasing before the war at the rate of twenty-five per cent. per annum, and as the growth of that great region has been even more rapid since that time in population and wealth, it seems fair that the consumption of coal has also increased, and must increase, I might almost say, indefinitely.

Again, not only does the market increase by increase of population, but there is a larger demand year by year from additions and improvements in the arts and manufactures ; for every new invention of a labor-saving machine usually implies a new source for the consumption of coal, either directly in the production of steam to run that machine, or indirectly in producing heat or steam for its manufacture, and ofttimes for both.

The salt formation extends from the Ohio toward the Alleghanies, but from lack of communication with market it has been heretofore but little explored, and its limits still less defined. In Mason County, in 1870, there were thirteen furnaces in operation, and before the war the manufacture of salt was carried on in a cheap way at Bulltown, Braxton County, and at Addison, in Webster County.

Its manufacture does not necessarily require a large capital, as the brine is obtained by putting down a bore till it reaches salt water, and putting in a small pump to pump it into reservoirs, whence it runs into the evaporating pans. In some cases the brine is brought up by the gas from the salt formation without the aid of pumps; and when this is the case, the gas is collected and forms a portion of the fuel by which the salt is made.

The timber along the line of your road is fine, and particularly so on the coal measures west of the Alleghanies, where the forests are unique in their magnificence. After spending some time in them one does not appreciate the size of the trees, but upon leaving the coal strata and going east, the trees there look dwarfish and stunted in comparison. All the varieties of oak, black and white walnut, wild cherry, hickory, poplar, beech, maple, chestnut, spruce, pine, etc. etc., abound; white oak three to three and a half feet in diameter and sixty feet to the first limbs; poplar four and six feet through and sixty and seventy feet to the crotch; hickory six and eight feet round and sixty feet long, and the other timbers on the same magnificent scale are common, while in Webster, Randolph, and Pocahontas Counties are large areas of wild cherry (so highly prized by cabinet-makers) four feet in diameter, seventy and eighty feet without a twig, and straight as an arrow. In some of these counties, owing to their inaccessibility to market, so little store is set by this timber, that one sees farm fences made of black walnut and wild cherry, and this valuable timber is burned to clear the land for small fields.

This region abounds in fine water-powers and manufacturing sites. The value of this will be better appreciated when it is called to mind that water-power is rated and paid for in other States at a yearly rent of from twenty to fifty dollars per horse-power, according to location and demand.

I would also make allusion to one peculiar feature incident to the small mountain creeks, which certainly can be found at but few other points. It is the use that can so easily be made of cheap hydraulic means for lifting and handling heavy weights. To illustrate: Many of the mountain streams can be turned into pipes with heads of (say) 300 feet, giving a pressure of (say) 125 pounds per square inch. Turn this water into a cylinder on a piston of eighteen inches, and allowing over thirty per cent. for friction, it will lift ten tons weight, and it can be operated by any one who can turn a hydrant cock.

This plan can be adopted in a hundred ways inexpensively, and with a saving of labor that in some instances amounts to a fair profit in itself. The idea of thus utilizing the water-fall of small streams in this country was first spoken of, I believe, by the Hon. Howell Fisher, M. E., of Pennsylvania.

The proposed Northern and Southern West Virginia Rail Road

will tap the Washington and Ohio Rail Road at Weston, Lewis County.

Along the Washington and Ohio Rail Road there is enough uncultivated land in Gilmer and Calhoun Counties for the settlement of large colonies; 75,000 to 80,000 acres may be obtained in a single tract for these purposes, and presents the unrivalled advantages of municipal government. They can worship at their own altar and educate their children by their own teachers, and all this in the healthiest country on the globe.

Lewis County is well adapted to the cereals, but lacking lines of communication abroad. We graze principally, and for that purpose there is no better land in the United States. Grapes, for wine, have recently been introduced, and succeed admirably.

The other counties along your road are similarly situated, but, with the exception of Mason, this is the best.

All children, who so desire, are educated in the free schools at public expense. The population of the county is about 12,000; it grazes 25,000 head of cattle; has sixteen post-offices; is traversed with turnpikes and good wagon roads; and there are public conveyances from one end of the county to the other. Weston is the county seat; it has a population of about 1600; has five churches and an academy. The insane asylum is also situated here; it has a frontage of 1235 feet, and will cost, when completed, one million dollars.

Your road will pass through the great petroleum belt. Some wells near the line are now being worked, yielding in the aggregate, perhaps, one thousand barrels per day. With improved lines of transportation, such as your road will furnish, it is just as easy to produce ten thousand barrels of oil per day as one, for all that is needed is the additional labor.

Much of the information here given was obtained from Professor M. F. Maury, Jr., (Geologist, etc., of this city. Professor Maury is a Fellow of the Geological Society of London, and a Graduate of the Royal School of Mines of England, as well as having the title of C.E. He is more thoroughly posted, I presume, as to the mineral, etc., wealth of this State than any other person within our borders, and for that reason I have drawn largely upon his store of information.

Yours, truly;

J. M. BENNETT.

PITTSTON, PA., December 5, 1872.

HON. LEWIS MCKENZIE,

President of W. and O. R. R., Alexandria, Va.

SIR: I have, by invitation, been on a visit to West Virginia, for the purpose of examining the coal-fields in the county of Randolph and a portion of Barbour County. The coal region in Randolph exceeds anything I have seen in this or any other country, and I have seen the most important coal districts in the States, from Pennsylvania to Nebraska. My acquaintance with bituminous coal dates back to my eleventh year, and my experience has been mostly in the counties of Northumberland and Durham, and in Newcastle, England. The coal veins, too, which we examined, would measure from thirty to thirty-five feet, and the most above or at water level, and, I may add, the nearest approach to the quality of Newcastle coal of any I have seen. The above veins would yield at least thirty thousand tons per acre; fifty acres per year would be one million five hundred thousand tons. The company that sent me to examine this coal-field have about four thousand acres, which is but a small part in the counties above named. On account of the lateness of the season, we did not make such an examination of the iron as we would like to have done, but, I have no doubt, it is in considerable quantity, as we found some good specimens. The timber is in abundance, and of large size and good quality—white and yellow poplar, cherry, different kinds of oak. The quality of the soil would warrant a large agricultural production of any kind; limestone in abundance and of good quality. In short, the above counties contain all the materials to make any community, with industry and sobriety, prosperous and wealthy. More might be said, and the whole not yet told. I have seen a notice in the *Christian Union*, giving a description of the material on the line of the Chesapeake and Ohio Rail Road. Without wishing to lessen in any degree what is stated in regard to the mineral wealth of those counties, the counties of Barbour and Randolph, in particular, far surpass, in my judgment, in coal and iron and limestone, anything in the line referred to. I have lived at the mouth of the Coal River, in Kanawha County, near two years, and I know what I state. As I have stated, the land and timber alone are worth the attention of capitalists and the poor man wanting a home. I would certainly prefer Western Virginia, with good timber and good soil, with good water and a healthy climate, to going west. I have no interest in making these statements, only to state what I have seen and is patent to any man of experience that wishes to see for himself.   Yours, respectfully,

JAMES M. BROWN.

The following article, from a late number of the "*Rockingham Register*," confirms the testimony (if confirmation were necessary) of Mr. Brown in relation to the heavy deposits of coal in Randolph County. Jack Mountain runs through Pendleton County for about twenty miles, and passes into Highland County, Va., on the south. Highland was formerly a part of Pendleton County. Doe Hill is a small settlement in Highland County.

MINERAL WEALTH.—Southwest of Harrisonburg, about thirty-five to forty miles, is a mountain, known as Bull Pasture Mountain. This mountain runs north and south, and is composed of three ridges. The first or main mountain has signs of iron ore to some extent; the second mountain, or ridge of Bull Pasture, is found to be a mountain of iron ore, or what is known as hydrated peroxyzed, or brown hematites. In many places this ore is found to crop out, and present a breast of pure hematite of not less than 200 yards wide, and extending for miles. This great body of iron ore extends on this Bull Pasture Mountain for a distance of some twenty miles; starting at Doe Hill, in Highland County, running south some twenty miles, near to the Bath County line; and west of this second ridge of the Bull Pasture Mountain adjoining, is the third ridge of mountain, which is composed of the purest limestone, an article so essential to the working to profit of this vast deposit of iron ore. Jack Mountain contains iron in as great quantities as the middle ridge of the Bull Pasture Mountain. All of this great iron deposit is well watered by the streams of Cow Pasture and Bull Pasture Rivers, with other live streams passing on west. These blossoms of iron extend to the county of Randolph, West Virginia, or near the head waters of the Elk River, at which are the great deposits of the finest coal, probably, now known on this continent. These great deposits of the fine fatty bituminous, the splint and the cannel coal, are found on the waters of Elk River in great abundance.

The distance from the end of the Orange, Alexandria and Manassas Rail Road at Harrisonburg, to the vast beds of iron in our sister county, is only about forty miles, and from the iron deposits we find these rich coal-fields only some forty miles west.—*Rockingham Register.*

Statistics of the Counties of Virginia through which the line of the Washington and Ohio Railroad passes. Compiled from the records of the year 1872.   By the Auditor of Public Accounts at Richmond.

COUNTIES.	Population in 1870.	Number of acres.	Value of real estate.	Value of live Stock.	Value of other property.	Total value.
Alexandria	13,570	.....	$3,497,710	$22,530	$1,334,674	$6,051,619
Alexandria County . . .	3,185	17,122	1,138,714	28,437	39,954	
Fairfax County . . .	12,952	252,027	5,092,656	359,587	694,507	6,146,750
Loudoun County . . .	22,893	324,722	12,219,112	975,757	1,619,808	14,814,687
Clarke County . . .	7,655	111,035	3,052,684	268,516	375,275	3,696,175
Winchester . . .	4,477	.....	1,274,537	.....	.....	......
Frederick County . . .	12,744	269,090	4,851,672	460,244	1,432,860	8,019,313
	77,476	973,996	$31,127,085	$2,114,781	$5,486,078	$38,728,544

Statistics of the Counties of the State of West Virginia through which the line of the Washington and Ohio Railroad passes, and those adjacent thereto. Compiled from the United States Census for the year 1870.

Counties.	Population in 1870.	Number of acres.	Value of real and personal estate.	Live Stock. Horses and mules.	Milch cows.	Sheep.	Hogs.	Other cattle.	Value.	Bushels of wheat.	Bushels of corn.	Bushels of oats.	Tons of hay.
Jefferson	16,562	110,667	$12,206,135	3,825	2,489	6,521	9,151	3,313	$561,038	476,456	336,287	41,077	5,753
Hampshire	8,125	256,144	2,531,198	2,415	2,673	8,317	4,763	3,884	381,454	76,832	120,325	46,769	4,557
Hardy	5,518	179,376	3,057,547	1,187	1,360	4,176	2,967	4,674	288,204	33,442	114,567	13,283	2,651
Grant	4,467	176,597	2,436,000	1,440	1,739	7,551	3,116	4,730	363,399	31,631	52,350	10,593	4,787
Pendleton	6,455	223,936	2,099,950	1,780	2,270	9,943	4,246	5,155	325,164	37,984	59,228	14,538	5,079
Tucker	1,907	66,005	505,285	501	637	2,608	1,045	1,084	112,583	1,469	27,813	14,726	1,498
Randolph	5,563	301,885	2,062,602	1,561	1,970	8,523	2,834	6,503	369,158	8,969	59,758	33,237	7,298
Barbour	10,312	216,524	3,882,280	3,182	3,622	11,738	6,501	8,068	658,275	42,303	173,195	43,367	10,503
Upshur	8,498	155,229	2,990,595	2,056	2,329	8,000	3,361	4,561	383,500	29,958	108,494	21,422	7,233
Braxton	6,480	186,543	2,000,000	1,588	2,049	9,923	6,513	2,105	218,990	20,019	130,690	29,908	1,951
Webster	1,730	69,653	551,005	266	643	2,018	1,136	769	49,677	1,196	21,075	4,689	504
Lewis	11,386	304,767	3,327,800	2,543	2,962	10,922	5,673	8,136	564,196	41,174	191,556	31,776	8,620
Harrison	16,714	283,783	8,500,000	5,107	4,906	15,852	8,951	15,855	1,267,287	83,473	327,261	56,183	16,901
Doddridge	7,076	149,108	2,567,551	1,848	1,987	7,183	3,304	2,782	300,950	15,879	113,064	18,723	4,649
Gilmer	4,512	117,874	919,133	1,124	1,295	6,100	3,907	1,637	162,509	9,830	106,036	17,592	1,636
Calhoun	2,961	78,824	577,791	517	666	3,232	1,741	904	81,350	5,382	52,202	8,357	985
Roane	7,375	250,651	1,469,196	1,583	1,858	12,973	7,112	3,477	241,585	24,087	160,912	28,489	3,013
Wirt	4,804	96,408	1,064,379	967	954	4,183	3,700	1,259	143,163	15,532	128,836	37,988	1,527
Jackson	10,888	150,301	2,514,026	2,622	2,289	13,610	8,821	3,644	370,271	59,815	272,044	48,524	2,934
Mason	20,811	153,436	7,900,000	2,725	2,332	9,880	9,879	5,183	544,564	115,350	456,990	43,464	4,353
	162,044	3,528,301	$63,162,773	38,937	41,030	163,213	99,321	87,783	$7,410,246	1,130,813	3,012,683	567,705	96,762

Distances on the Washington and Ohio Railroad from Alexandria.
(From Washington by the present junction it is 4 miles further.)

To Falls Church	10½ miles.
Vienna	15 "
Hunter's Mill	18 "
Thornton	21 "
Herndon	23¼ "
Guilford	27 "
Farmwell	31 "
Leesburg	37½ "
Clark's Gap	41½ "
Hamilton	44 "
Purcellville	47½ "
Round Hill	50 "
Snickersville	54¾ "
Berryville	64 "
Winchester	75 "
Rock Enon Spring	90 "
Capon Springs	95 "
Baker's Run	111¾ "
Summit South Branch Mountain	120½ "
Moorefield	131¾ "
Petersburg	142¼ "
Summit of the Alleghany	166¾ "
Forks Red Creek (Coal Lands)	172¾ "
Buckhannon	224¾ "
Weston	239¾ "
Glenville	250 "
Little Kanawha River	266¾ "
West Fork of Little Kanawha	289¾ "
Sandyville	315¾ "
Point Pleasant (on the Ohio)	325 "

Distances Saved by the Washington and Ohio Railroad from Cincinnati to Eastern Cities.

FROM CINCINNATI TO			Washington and Ohio Railroad.	Saved by Washington and Ohio Railroad.
Boston	*via*	New York Central and connections	939 miles.	940 miles.	154 miles.
New York	*via*	Erie Railroad and connections . . .	860 "	706 "	154 miles.
New York	*via*	New York Central and connections .	883 "	706 "	177 "
New York	*via*	Pennsylvania Central and connections	744 "	706 "	38 "
New York	*via*	Baltimore and Ohio Railroad and connections .	777 "	706 "	71 "
Philadelphia	*via*	Pennsylvania Central and connections	668 "	619 "	49 "
Philadelphia	*via*	Baltimore and Ohio Railroad and connections .	686 "	619 "	67 "
Baltimore	*via*	Pennsylvania Central and connections .	647 "	521 "	126 "
Baltimore	*via*	Baltimore and Ohio Railroad and connections .	588 "	521 "	67 "
Washington	*via*	Pennsylvania Central and connections .	687 "	483 "	204 "
Washington	*via*	Baltimore and Ohio and Metropolitan Branch and connections .	560 "	483 "	77 "
Washington	*via*	Baltimore and Ohio and Washington Branch and connections .	610 "	483 "	127 "

www.ingramcontent.com/pod-product-compliance
Lightning Source LLC
Chambersburg PA
CBHW021409090426
42742CB00009B/1074